The West Point Fitness and Diet Book

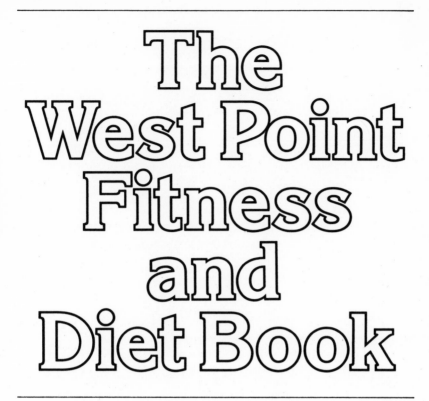

The West Point Fitness and Diet Book

**Colonel James L. Anderson
and
Martin Cohen**

Rawson Associates Publishers, Inc.
New York

Illustrations by Marie Zimmerman

Library of Congress Cataloging in Publication Data
Anderson, James Lee, 1933–
  The West Point fitness and diet book.
  1. Exercise.   2. Physical fitness.   3. Reducing
diets.   I. Cohen, Martin Aver, joint author.
II. Title.
RA781.A594   1977   613.7   76–43424
ISBN 0–89256–008–8

Published simultaneously in Canada by McClelland and
Stewart, Ltd.
Manufactured in the United States of America
by The Book Press, Brattleboro, Vermont
Designed by Gene Siegel
First Edition

For Joyce, Terri, and David
J.L.A.

For Mary, Peter, Tom, and Jim
M.C.

Contents

WARNING: Check with your physician before beginning the exercise and diet program. A person who has been inactive for a long time, smokes, or is significantly overweight may require a medical examination, and the physician may also want to modify the program.

The symbols below are used in the exercise portions of this book to indicate that the exercises are for both male and female or for the entire family.

Men and Women 18 to 50 Plus

Younger Children

The Later Years

The Teen Years

Entire Family

INTRODUCTION

The World's Best Conditioning Program

". . . the world's best conditioning program . . ."

You can skip this introduction and turn directly to the basic conditioning plans. The program is graded safely by sex and age groups. The instructions are simple and precise. Nothing is left to chance. This is likely to be the best physical fitness program that you have ever used.

The West Point program is unique for a combination of reasons:

• It is honest and totally absent in gimmickry, false implications, and faddist nonsense.

• It assumes that you are an average, normal person who has been getting little or no exercise. Conditioning is gradual, designed to avoid both fatigue and the muscular soreness that could interfere with your usual workday and social life.

• It is a dynamic program. Conditioning progresses through three levels. If you think your fitness level is higher than a beginner's, plug in at an appropriate higher level.

• It is designed to be adapted to your particular needs. *You* decide how much fitness is useful to you, and you learn how to personally monitor your progress.

• It is a medically sound program. The West Point Diet is safe and virtually foolproof. The conditioning plans contain only quality exercises—those exercises that are comprehensive and efficient in conditioning primary muscle groups.

• And most important, we know the program works. It is an adaptation of the personal conditioning program that has been successful for over three decades and for more than 20,000 cadets, and it continues to serve them through their middle years.

The basic goals of the cadets at West Point are the same as

those of many other men and women—to develop muscle tone, a trim figure, good health, and the endurance to meet work stress at a peak performance level. The major difference is only in the degree of conditioning. A cadet or officer must be physically prepared for combat and rigorous field duty. Since the average man and woman doesn't need that much conditioning, you need not work as hard as the cadets, although this book gives you the option of increasing your condition to as high a level as you desire.

Do You Need the Program?

This is not a hit-or-miss program. There's no chance of your being frustrated, because the program delivers exactly what it promises. The conditioning plans for all age groups are designed to guarantee the following specific results, which you may use as a checklist to determine your needs:

• Tone up your muscles to improve your posture and figure.

• Reduce inches in the waistline, abdomen, hips, thighs, and upper arms.

• Help trim off body fat when implemented with the West Point Diet Plan.

• Improve the health of your heart, blood vessels, and lungs for longer life and increased daily vigor.

• Maintain the flexibility necessary for coordination, grace, and the prevention of lower-back pain and joint injuries.

• Increase your stamina to meet life's demands and to take advantage of life's opportunities.

And stamina is an essential benefit of physical fitness.

For the youngster stamina means building up strength and endurance to get through a school day, a ball game after school, and then an evening of homework, recreation, or other special activity.

For the adult from 18 through the middle years it means doing a day's job without headaches and midafternoon exhaustion and having a reservoir of energy for an evening of tennis, dating, bowling, a class in modern dance or economic analysis— or just having the verve to enjoy friends and family.

For the retiree it means maintaining the pride and self-respect that comes from physical independence.

Physical fitness depends on comprehensive conditioning that

can't be found in any single sport or any physical occupation, whether it be ditch digging or spring house cleaning. But what is physical fitness?

What Makes Up Good Basic Fitness?

1. *Weight control and proper nutrition* are basic components of fitness. Being overweight is not just a matter of appearance—obesity is a drag, a handicap, and a killer. Every pound of excess fat requires 4,500 feet of blood-vessel and capillary expansion that places a tremendous extra work load on the heart, making every extra pound a high-risk factor in heart disease and heart attacks.

2. *Flexibility,* achieved and maintained through stretching exercises, is another prime component of fitness. Flexibility is the ability to move a joint through a normal range of motion. Poor flexibility can be responsible for joint injuries, lower-back pain, poor posture, and ordinary muscular soreness.

3. *Muscular strength*—the force required to perform an act one time—is a third component of good fitness. It could be lifting a barbell or a toothbrush, striking the key of a piano or typewriter, or putting one foot forward to take a step. It is also this strength that helps overcome abdominal or bust sag and allows us to sit and stand upright.

4. *Muscular endurance,* another prime component, is the quality that enables us to hit that piano key, lift that barbell, and take that step over and over and over. And it is muscular endurance that helps us maintain a good posture throughout the day.

5. All of the preceding components are important to basic physical fitness, but the most critical in staying alive is *cardiorespiratory efficiency*. It is cardiorespiratory fitness that helps prevent a heart attack or stroke.

The cardiorespiratory (CR) system consists of the lungs (respiratory organs), which take in oxygen and pass the oxygen into the heart, and the blood vessels (vascular system), which carry the blood with its nutrients and oxygen throughout the body. If the system fails, you have a heart attack, and about 50 percent of heart attacks end in sudden death. If oxygen fails to reach your brain, you have a stroke that may result in death or paralysis.

These are the critical reasons for maintaining CR efficiency. However, a poorly conditioned cardiorespiratory system can also be the cause of general inefficiency in our daily lives. For example, when you become physically exhausted in a game or other physical activity, when your heart pounds and your breathing is labored, the problem is not muscular fatigue but the inability of the system to deliver enough oxygen.

What many people don't understand is that like a muscle group the cardiorespiratory system can be conditioned to perform more efficiently through exercises. Conditioning helps maintain the elasticity of the blood vessels. Conditioning strengthens and enlarges the heart so that it will pump more blood per beat, which means that the heart does not have to work as hard to maintain blood circulation. And it's also believed that conditioning may promote the growth of additional vessels, which take over the role of the narrowing main coronary vessels that feed the heart.

These are the five major components that contribute to a lifetime of good health and appearance. The question is: What will conditioning cost you in time and work?

Is the Program Difficult? Easy?

You won't have to be either a contortionist or an acrobat. None of the exercises is difficult. However, each exercise is designed to put a little stress on a group of muscles or the cardiorespiratory system. The basic principle of obtaining physical fitness is stress or overload. If you overload muscles and the CR system little by little every day or every other day, your body tone and health improves gradually and safely.

The amount of required stress is moderate. If the exercise is easy, if you feel relaxed and comfortable, you are wasting your time. On the other hand, you don't want to either strain or tire yourself. When you feel fatigue coming on, take a brief rest between exercises. You'll find that you can do more in the long run.

Remember, too, that none of the conditioning plans should be considered either games or sport. Don't compare your running or exercise records with the family or a friend. Individuals move along at their own rate when conditioning, and if you try to compete, you are liable to hurt yourself.

Is the Program Permissive?

Permissive is a dirty word to some people. This is not our attitude at West Point. New cadets are taught exercises that are necessary for personal conditioning, just as you will learn conditioning by reading the book. From that time on, cadets are on their own. Cadets are not, as some believe, hauled out at reveille to go through calisthenics, nor does anyone oversee cadets when they work out in the gymnasium or their quarters. The decisions and responsibility to maintain fitness is that of the individual cadet.

On the other hand, we don't allow that kind of permissiveness that appears in some fitness programs—the notion that there are easy substitutes for specific exercises; that instead of doing designated exercises to develop the upper torso, you merely need to shake that saltshaker a little harder or toast your friends a little more vigorously when you lift a beer mug; or that to improve your cardiorespiratory system, all you have to do is yawn and take deep breaths when you ride an elevator.

Permissive?

Yes, in that we will not tell you how far you should go in conditioning. How much fitness is your decision.

Permissive?

No, in that we do not recommend that you make up your own alternatives to some exercises. The kind of exercise and the method of doing it will be precise because we know what works.

How Much Time Will It Take?

Some programs are sold to the public on a time basis, claiming that you can get total fitness and/or total health in 5 or 3 minutes a day; in fact one promises "instant fitness." Such programs are a total hustle. There's no way you can cover basic conditioning in 5 minutes a day, let alone in the blink of an eyelid. On the West Point program, you will have the choice of putting in from 15 to 45 minutes a day.

Fifteen minutes is just about the minimum satisfactory. If you want faster progress, you can increase your daily conditioning to 30 or 45 minutes. The decision is all yours. However, once you have the basic plans working for you, we think you should begin to think about putting some of that conditioning into fun. For some ideas you should then turn to Chapter 13, Lifetime Sports.

The 15-Minute, Million-Dollar Reward

If we are honest with ourselves, we have to admit that anyone can spare 15 minutes a day for good health. When we complain that we don't have time to exercise, we are really trying to make an excuse for our inertia. The problem: Muscles are lazy. You must consciously order muscles to exercise, and that takes a little effort. Rather than overcome this inertia, some adults resist conditioning just as a child may resist doing homework because he will have to work at it.

To overcome inertia, to put muscles to work, we usually expect a reward. The reward in conditioning is feeling "like a million." You will look and feel good, sleep better, eliminate a lot of ordinary aches and pains, and be able to ignore the TV commercials on regularity.

You can expect early returns and rewards. If you tend to wake up stiff, the Basic Five will work out that soreness before you go to work. If you're a slow waker, then early-morning exercises will get you alert sooner. Within ten days you will begin to develop a comfortable rhythm and swing. You will walk taller and lighter and run for the bus without choking for breath. By the fourth week you will begin to see an improvement in your posture, and by the sixth week a reduction in your girth. By the time you have reached the maintenance level, you will discover that you have developed a new habit: You will feel compelled to exercise because now you know how great it is to feel healthy and look good.

How can we be so sure?

We are experts in the science of physical fitness. At West Point we have to be.

SECTION I

Personal Conditioning Program for Men and Women Ages 18 to 50 Plus

CHAPTER 1

Getting Started

This program has been designed for normal, working adults from the ages of 18 to 50 plus. The program progresses gradually to prevent your suffering fatigue or soreness that could interfere with your workday or social life. It assumes that your life is largely sedentary, with little or no exercise. This includes the executive who plays weekend golf and tennis and also the housewife who swings a mop and broom, because neither recreational sports nor housework is comprehensive in conditioning.

What It Will Do for You

The goals of the program are all attainable and specific. The direct benefits include:

Vigor. The program increases your strength and endurance to ensure that you get through your workday feeling strong and alert, with enough reserve energy for an evening of chess, dancing, tennis, bowling, or sitting attentively through a class lecture.

Appearance. Whether you are in your late twenties or your late fifties, you will shed that middle-aged look. The program will tone up muscles to slenderize your body at the waist, hips, and buttocks, strengthen your legs and upper shoulders, firm your bustline, tighten up abdominal muscles to hold in your stomach, and help prevent lower-back pain. When the exercises are coordinated with the diet plan, you will have a safe and sound way to lose body fat permanently.

Health. Your quality of life will improve through better health. You will sleep better, feel less tension. You will be able to cope with stress and shock through cardiorespiratory conditioning. You will reduce risk of injury in sports and housework with improved muscular tone and flexibility. As your body sheds that middle-aged look, you will literally slow down the aging process by ten or more years.

How the Program Works

The program is adapted from the personal conditioning program that works for the cadets. You won't work as hard as the cadets because you don't need that much conditioning. However, to achieve similar overall fitness depends on your following four plans:

The Basic Five. Four of the Basic Five exercises condition the primary muscle groups. The fifth exercise improves the efficiency of lungs, blood vessels, and the heart. It is a minimum exercise for the cardiorespiratory system, which you can discontinue when you get into the Walk/Run Plan, Chapter 3.

Walk/Run. If you followed only one plan, this is the one that many health professionals would choose. The Walk/Run Plan is the most efficient way to condition your cardiorespiratory system, which is life itself. The immediate results are increased stamina and vigor. The long-term results are a fuller, longer, and healthier life.

Flexibility. Most of us begin to lose flexibility when we begin to sit for long periods in school or at work. The loss of flexibility is a slow, subtle, but steady process, and it accounts for stiffness and soreness in joints and muscles and for over 80 percent of that national nemesis, lower-back pain. In Chapter 4, (page 55) you'll find easy tests to check your flexibility and exercises to bring back normal flexibility.

Weight Control. If you're fat, you know it. If you're not sure, take off your clothes, stand in front of a mirror, and keep your eyes open. If you are still uncertain, check with your physician and/or the desirable-weights chart in Chapter 5, Weight Control and Nutrition, which also includes a sound diet.

How to Get Started

Take off your shoes and begin with the Basic Five. Afterward turn to Chapter 4, Flexibility. In some cases the test and exercise are identical. All are simple, and each takes less than a minute.

Take your time in preparing for the Walk/Run Plan because this is the most important commitment you will make. The plan itself is intriguing because you will be monitoring your own progress by recording your pulse rate. For many this will be their first insight into the function of the lungs, blood vessels, and heart.

Finally, if you need to slim down, the Weight Control Plan includes an absolutely safe and foolproof diet that is compassionate and relatively easy to use. And if you don't know what your desirable weight should be, Chapter 5 will tell you.

Once you've looked over the different plans, the matter of scheduling comes up. You can schedule exercising for any time of day or night except during the first full hour after a meal. The next question is how much time you will allot. This can't be exact because it depends on your age and level of conditioning. However, here are some estimates that tend toward the maximum time required:

The Basic Five: 12 to 15 minutes a day. You can shorten this by eliminating the cardiorespiratory exercise (the fifth in the Basic Five) on those days when you walk/run.

Walk/Run: Depending on age and level, this will take 12 to 30 minutes. The object here is maintaining your pulse rate at 60 to 70 percent of maximum for 5 to 12 minutes. During the time you are walking (catching your breath), your pulse will drop below the conditioning level. However, after you've reached the maintenance level, you should be able to run 12 minutes straight at 60 to 70 percent of maximum, and that will be all the time required for cardiorespiratory conditioning.

Flexibility: These are literally no-sweat exercises that take less than a minute each. You can do them one at a time when you take a coffee break or stretch at home or at work. On the other hand, if you wish to schedule Flexibility by time, allow a total of 5 minutes.

In the beginning, when you are learning, everything takes a little longer. By the second or third week, you will be surprised at how quickly you swing through the schedule efficiently and easily. Now let's talk about specific schedules.

THE IDEAL SCHEDULE

Mon.	Tues.	Wed.	Thurs.	Fri.	Sat.
B-Five	B-Five	B-Five	B-Five	B-Five	B-Five
W/R	W/R	W/R	W/R	W/R	W/R
Flex.	Flex.	Flex.	Flex.	Flex.	Flex.

If you follow the above schedule, remember that you don't have to do it all at one time. You could schedule the Basic Five in the morning before going to work or school. Choose any time for the Flexibility exercises. You can do the Walk/Run at midday or in the evening. Using the above schedule, the total exercises, not including Flexibility, will take 24 to 45 minutes a day. If you include Flexibility, the range is 29 to 50 minutes a day. If you wish to modify the above schedule, you could cut down the Basic Five to three alternate days a week. In that case you will stay on each level in the progression chart twice as long.

THE SATISFACTORY SCHEDULE

Mon.	Tues.	Wed.	Thurs.	Fri.	Sat.
B-Five	W/R	B-Five	W/R	B-Five	W/R
Flex.	Flex.	Flex.	Flex.	Flex.	Flex.

Using the above schedule, you will cut your time considerably. On three days a week you will be doing the Basic Five, which will take you 12 to 15 minutes. The other three days you will be doing the Walk/Run, which will take 12 to 30 minutes, depending on your condition and age. Understand that you are not cheating yourself by working out according to the Satisfactory Schedule. And you shouldn't feel guilty about not doing enough. In fact, the conditioning will be just as effective as with the Ideal Schedule, but it will take longer. You should spend twice as much time at each level but, in the end, you will arrive at the same maintenance level.

THE ABSOLUTE MINIMUM

Mon.	Tues.	Wed.	Thurs.	Fri.	Sat.
W/R		W/R		W/R	

The above schedule is absolute-minimum conditioning for the cardiorespiratory system. It will do nothing for flexibility and nothing for toning up muscles except for those in the legs.

For information on correct clothing and shoes, proper breathing and running, etc., see Chapter 12, Tips for Better Performance. For information especially pertinent to the physical fitness of women, see Chapter 14, For Women Only.

CHAPTER 2

The Basic Five

Four of the Basic Five exercises cover the primary muscle groups. Conditioning these muscles will increase strength and muscular endurance, improve appearance and posture, and help eliminate muscular soreness—in short, make you look and feel good. The four categories of primary muscles are:

Abdominal

Trunk (waist)

Thighs, hips, buttocks, lower back

Arms, chest, shoulders

The fifth exercise is Walk/Run-in-Place, minimum conditioning for the cardiorespiratory system until you begin the full Walk/Run plan.

The program is designed to minimize strain, but you can further reduce the possibility of soreness and undue fatigue by remaining at any level of the Basic Five until you feel that you are ready to move on. Also, if you don't like any single exercise, you can continue with the previous one in the same category.

Preferably, you should maintain a six-day schedule. Next best, and satisfactory, would be three alternate days a week. On the alternate-day schedule spend two weeks at each progression. As you become familiar with the Basic Five, the program will take 10 to 15 minutes, depending on your mood and level of energy.

Some Questions About the Basic Five

Q. *When is the best time to exercise?*

A. Any time of the day, but wait an hour after a meal. Early morning is recommended, before breakfast and a shower, because it is too easy to make excuses later in the day. Turning the radio to upbeat music or the news can help relieve boredom.

Q. *What if I feel too tired to exercise?*

A. Contrary to the general notion, moderate exercising is energizing and will pick you up. Sometimes exercise can overcome chronic fatigue. So give it a chance. If, however, you find that you are exhausted, put exercising off until the next day.

Q. *What do these exercises have to do with combating fatigue?*

A. The human body is not very stable. In order to maintain an upright position our muscles are always fighting the pull of gravity, and these are the muscles that fatigue as we go through a normal day. You can see older people who do no muscle conditioning lose the fight to gravity as their bodies bend and shorten. So conditioning the antigravity muscles, which are mostly in the abdomen, trunk, buttocks, and front of the thigh, not only helps maintain good posture but also gives you the muscular endurance to get through the day without collapsing.

Q. *How hard should I exercise?*

A. If you feel comfortable and relaxed while exercising, you are wasting time. Without stress, muscles will not strengthen. So you must exert yourself. However, the stress should be minimal, particularly in the beginning. Never work to the point of exhaustion. There is a difference between straining and working with moderate vigor. (For special information on correct breathing, regulation of body temperature, etc., see Chapter 12, Tips for Better Performance.)

Q. *Under what circumstances should I stop exercising?*

A. If you feel unusually sore at the end of the first day of exercising, then skip one day and start out again with a reduced number of exercises until the soreness is gone and then begin increasing gradually to a higher level. Also, if illness interrupts your exercise schedule, start up again at a lower level.

Q. *How soon will I see results?*

A. Within four to six weeks you should feel the results in body toning and see an improvement in posture. You may also take body measurements when you begin the program and at six-week intervals. (See diagram and instructions in Chapter 6, Testing and Recording Your Progress.)

Q. *If I'm playing tennis, handball, golf, or any other game, should I pass up the Basic Five for that day?*

A. No. Although sports are strongly recommended, virtually no other physical activity, including ditchdigging or a hard day of housework, is as comprehensive in reaching the primary muscles.

Q. *Why do I need the Basic 5 when I get exercise working in the yard?*

A. Raking leaves, gardening or even taking long walks isn't enough. For example, you could be a vigorous walker but you may not be able to do one push-up because walking doesn't develop the muscles in your upper torso.

Curiously, a national study finds that most persons who think they get enough exercise in their own activities really don't. The activity is not comprehensive in covering the primary muscle groups. So check yourself out. Test yourself on the Basic 5. If you can't perform these exercises at the maintenance level for your age group then you are out of condition.

Q. *In what way will these exercises make me feel better?*

A. Besides combating fatigue as explained above, the Basic 5 will help reduce muscular tension caused by worry and other emotional pressures. Exercise relieves this tension and is kind of an "emotional safety valve."

Q. *Should a woman exercise during menopause, pregnancy or menstrual periods?*

A. Contrary to the myths, most women benefit from exercise during menopause, menstrual periods, and pregnancy. The Basic 5 not only helps a woman maintain her general health but also helps reduce some of the discomfort that derives from muscular tension. (For further information on myths that handicap women, see Chapter 14.)

Q. *Can I do the Basic 5 if I suffer with backaches?*

A. Studies find that you can usually get rid of aches and pain in the lower back with proper exercise. This has been taken into account in designing the Basic 5 and Flexibility exercises. As a result, the ordinary and most common kind of lower back pain should vanish. If the pain continues or if the pain is severe in doing exercises, you should speak to your physician.

Q. *Will I lose weight with the Basic Five?*

A. You may lose inches from the waistline, thighs, hips, and upper arms as you tone your muscles, but if you have to lose a dramatic amount of weight, the most efficient way is dieting. (See Chapter 5, Weight Control and Nutrition.)

To actually work off fat without dieting requires an intolerable amount of exercise. For example, a 150-pound person would have to walk about 58 miles to lose 1 pound, which is not to say that you shouldn't. If you walk 2 miles a day, or preferably walk/run for your heart, you'll lose a pound a month, or 12 pounds in a year. And that's all to the good. Exercising along with dieting is the best way to lose weight.

Also, exercise is an important aid to dieting. Contrary to the popular notion, moderate exercising actually moderates your appetite and helps you to counteract overeating. On the other hand, studies always find that when people are sedentary, most of them overeat. Farmers use this gambit by penning up animals they want to fatten.

Q. *Can I use some of these exercises to spot-reduce?*

A. Spot reducing is a hoax. It is impossible to wear off fat or rub off fat at any particular spot through exercises, massage, or wishful thinking. Exercising takes up the slack in muscles. Dieting takes off the fat.

Q. *Why are there two sets of exercises, one for men and one for women?*

A. Since many women have not been encouraged to develop fitness through sports activities during their early years, by the time they are young adults, they lack the muscular strength and endurance of men. This accounts for the difference in the exercises. (If you read the chapter on younger children or the chapter addressed to teen-agers, you will see that we hope to correct this inequity.) Of course, if a woman feels that she's in good condition, she should use the men's exercises. Or she can switch to them when she reaches the maintenance level in her category. (For special information on women and fitness, see Chapter 14, For Women Only.)

Q. *What if I find the exercises too easy?*

A. You can easily adapt the plan to your needs if you understand the overload principle, which is basic to conditioning. The principle is simple: To increase muscular strength and endurance you must moderately stress a muscle. You do this by moving onto a more stressful exercise or by increasing the repetitions.

If you find an exercise in the beginning level too easy, then try the intermediate or maintenance level. Or if you are in your fifties but in good condition, you can work at a lower age level.

If you are in your twenties, you may want to try the teen-age routines, which are more difficult.

And you have another option: If you want to go beyond the maintenance level, then you can move on to Chapter 10, BBC—Beyond Basic Conditioning where you will find three comprehensive exercise routines that you can substitute for the Basic Five.

Q. *Is it a good idea to exercise with the family or with friends?*

A. Any idea that is motivating or makes exercising less of a bore is good. However, you must remember that the personal conditioning program is noncompetitive. You shouldn't compare yourself with a friend, spouse, or child. You progress at your own rate safely and soundly. That is what a personal conditioning program is all about.

Q. *Can I stop exercising after I've reached the maintenance level?*

A. No. Physical conditioning cannot be stored. By the time you reach the maintenance level, the rewards will motivate you to keep working. Remember that in addition to such obvious benefits as better health and better looks, a maintenance program slows down the aging process and helps you cope with crises, accidents, and disease at any age.

After reaching the maintenance level, you may design a program to meet your own needs for physical fitness by choosing an exercise from each of the other four categories. You should continue to exercise no less than three days a week, on alternate days.

There are three exercises that are common to both sexes and appear on the following pages:

1. The warm-up exercises, which precede the Basic Five

2. The cooling-off exercises, which follow the Basic Five

3. The walk/run-in-place exercise for cardiorespiratory conditioning.

WARM-UP EXERCISES
(MEN AND WOMEN—ALL LEVELS)

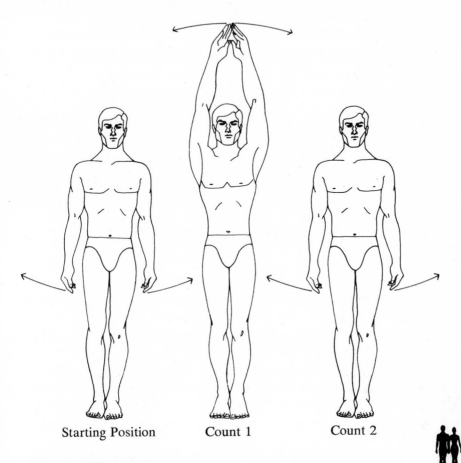

Starting Position   Count 1   Count 2

Overhead Stretch

Purpose: To limber up before doing the Basic Five.

Starting Position: Stand at attention.

Action: Count 1. In single motion, rise on toes while swinging arms sideward and then upward, touching hands above head. Stretch body while rising, tuck in buttocks and abdomen.

Count 2. Return to starting position.

Repetitions: About 15 times in approximately 30 seconds.

Cadence: Slow.

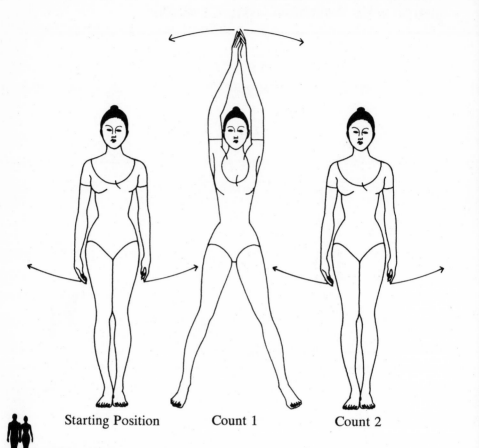

Starting Position   Count 1   Count 2

Jumping Jack

Purpose: To limber up before doing the Basic Five.

Starting Position: Stand at attention.

Action: Count 1. Jump off both feet simultaneously, spreading feet and landing on toes a little more than shoulder width apart. At the same time, swing arms sideward and then upward over your head.

Count 2. Spring back to starting position.

Repetitions: About 30 jumps in approximately 30 seconds.

Cadence: Start slowly. Gradually increase pace.

NOTE: Some persons over 50 may prefer to do only the overhead stretch for one minute.

COOLING-OFF EXERCISE
(MEN AND WOMEN—ALL LEVELS)

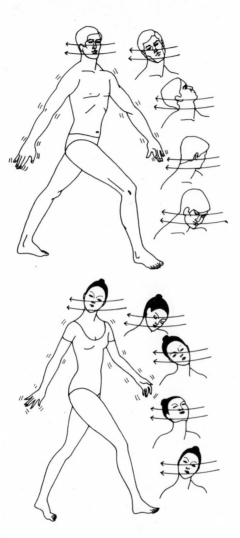

Shakedown

Purpose: To cool off after exercising.

Starting Position: Body loose, posture unimportant.

Action: Walk around the room with exaggeratedly long steps, stretching legs and hamstring muscles while at the same time shaking your arms and hands along your side and rolling head. Continue until relaxed and heart rate is normal.

CARDIORESPIRATORY EXERCISES (MEN AND WOMEN—ALL LEVELS)

Walk-in-Place   *Run-in-Place*   *Skip Rope, Boxer's Style*

Walk-in-Place

Purpose: To improve health of lungs, blood vessels, and heart.

Starting Position: Stand at attention.

Action: Walk vigorously, toes pointed forward. As endurance builds, increase speed and raise knees higher.

Run-in-Place

Starting Position: Stand erect, on your toes with feet pointed forward.

Action: Run in place, raising feet four to six inches off the floor. As endurance builds, increase speed and raise knees higher. (Run in place on carpeted or padded floor. When in excess of two minutes, wear tennis or running shoes.)

NOTE: Rope skipping may be substituted for Run-in-Place. If you can, use boxer's style. If you can't, use any rope-skipping style that you can maintain at a constant tempo.

Skip Rope, Boxer's Style

Starting Position: Stand erect, feet together, on toes.

Action: Jump, with both feet leaving the floor at the same time, rope passing under both feet, and both feet returning to the floor simultaneously. Increase tempo as endurance builds.

MEN'S BASIC FIVE PROGRESSION CHART
(Beginning Level — Four Weeks)

Week	Abdomen Bent-Knee Half-Curl				Trunk (Waist) Body Bender				Thighs, Hips, Buttocks, Lower Back Half Knee Bend				Arms, Shoulders, Chest Modified Push-up				Cardiorespiratory System Walk/Run-in-Place or Skip Rope
	1st	2nd	3rd	4th	1st	2nd	3rd	4th	1st	2nd	3rd	4th	1st	2nd	3rd	4th	
Ages 18–29	10	12	16	20	12	14	16	20	12	14	16	20	12	14	16	20	Run for 3 min. Gradually increase to 4 min. / Skip rope for 1 min. Gradually increase to 3 min.
Ages 30–39	8	10	13	16	10	12	15	18	10	12	15	18	10	12	15	18	Run 1 min. Gradually increase to 3 min. / Skip rope for 30 sec. Increase to 2 min.
Ages 40–49	6	8	10	12	8	10	12	14	8	10	12	14	8	10	12	14	Run ½ min. Increase gradually to 2 min. / Skip rope 20 sec. Increase to 1 min. 30 sec.
Age 50 plus	4	5	6	8	6	7	8	10	6	7	8	10	6	7	8	10	Walk in place for 3 min.

NOTE: Figures in boxes represent the number of repetitions.

MEN'S BEGINNING LEVEL
Category: **Abdomen**

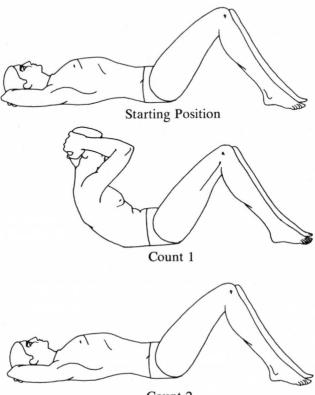

Starting Position

Count 1

Count 2

Bent-Knee Half-Curl

Starting Position: Lie on back. Heels on floor. Knees bent at about a 45- to 90-degree angle. Hands interlaced behind head.

Action: Count 1. Tucking chin into your chest, slowly curl forward until your shoulders are about ten inches off the floor. Hold position off floor for count of three seconds.

Count 2. Slowly return to starting position.

Cadence: Slow.

Category: **Trunk (Waist)**

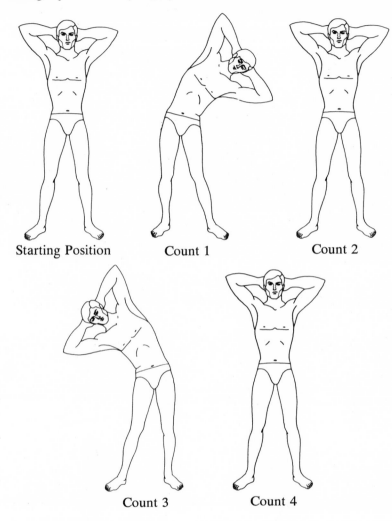

Starting Position   Count 1   Count 2

Count 3   Count 4

Body Bender

Starting Position: Stand with feet about shoulder width apart. Hands interlaced behind head. Elbows back.

Action: Count 1. Bend trunk sideward to left as far as possible.
Count 2. Return to starting position.
Count 3. Bend trunk to right as far as possible.
Count 4. Return to starting position.

Cadence: Moderate.

Category: **Thighs, Hips, Buttocks, Lower Back**

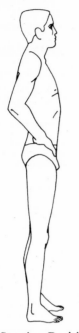

Starting Position

Count 1

Count 2

Half Knee Bend

Starting Position: Stand with feet six to eight inches apart. Hands
on hips.

Action: Count 1. Bend knees to half-squat position while simultaneously swinging arms forward with
palms down.
Count 2. Return to starting position.

Cadence: Moderate.

Category: **Arms, Shoulders, Chest**

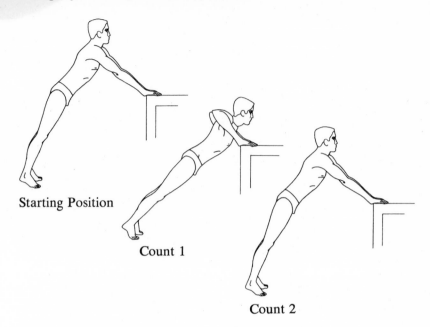

Starting Position

Count 1

Count 2

Modified Push-up

Starting Position: Place hands about shoulder width apart on front edge of bed (or sturdy chair or bench). Now move your feet backward until your legs and back are in a straight line, your body weight being supported only by your feet and your hands.

Action: Count 1. Keeping your head up, bend arms at elbow and lower your body until your chest touches front edge of bed.

              Count 2. Push up, straightening arms until you have returned to starting position.

Cadence: Moderate.

NOTE: If this exercise is too easy, you can do push-ups off a hassock or stool or, for maximum stress, off the floor. If the exercise is too difficult, then push off a desk, table, kitchen counter, or for the least stress, the side of a wall. Understand that the higher your hands are placed, the less body weight you are lifting. For progressive conditioning of the upper torso, you literally work your way down to floor push-ups. When pushing off a chair, stool, bench, etc., place furniture against wall for added support and safety.

MEN'S BASIC FIVE PROGRESSION CHART
(Intermediate Level — Four Weeks)

Week	Abdomen				Trunk (Waist)				Thighs, Hips, Buttocks, Lower Back				Arms, Shoulders, Chest				Cardiorespiratory System
	Bent-Knee Curl				Trunk Twister				Hip Raise				Classic Push-up				Walk/Run-in-Place or Skip Rope
	1st	2nd	3rd	4th	1st	2nd	3rd	4th	1st	2nd	3rd	4th	1st	2nd	3rd	4th	
Ages 18–29	18	22	26	30	12	14	16	20	10	12	14	16	12	16	20	25	Run in place 4 min. Increase to 6 min. Skip rope 3 min. Increase to 5 min.
Ages 30–39	16	18	22	26	10	12	15	18	8	10	12	14	10	13	16	20	Run in place 3 min. Increase to 5 min. Skip rope 2 min. Increase to 4 min.
Ages 40–49	12	14	17	20	8	10	12	14	6	8	10	10	8	10	12	15	Run in place 2 min. Increase to 4 min. Skip rope 1 min. 30 sec. Increase to 3 min.
Ages 50 plus	Continue bent-knee half-curls 8	10	12	14	6	7	8	10	4	5	6	8	Continue with modified push-ups 4	6	8	10	Run in place 30 sec. Walk 1 min. Repeat 2 times.

NOTE: Figures in boxes represent the number of repetitions.

MEN'S INTERMEDIATE LEVEL
Category: **Abdomen**

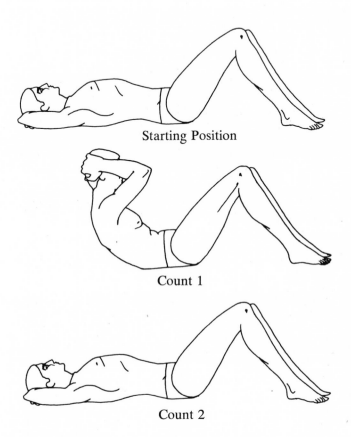

Starting Position

Count 1

Count 2

Bent-Knee Curl

Starting Position: Lie on back with knees bent at an angle of 45
to 90 degrees. Hands interlaced behind head.

> Count 1. Tucking chin into chest, curl forward into
> a sitting position until you can touch your
> elbows to your knees.
> Count 2. Return to the starting position.

Cadence: Start slowly and gradually increase pace.

Category: **Trunk (Waist)**

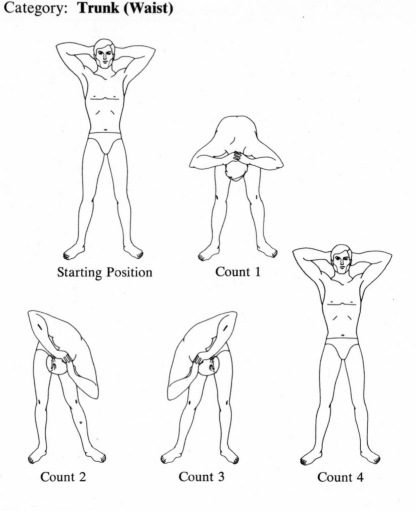

Starting Position   Count 1

Count 2   Count 3   Count 4

Trunk Twister

Starting Position: Stand with feet separated about shoulder
    width. Head up. Hands interlaced behind back.
    Throughout this exercise keep legs straight and elbows
    back.

> Count 1. Bend forward to waist level.
> Count 2. Twist trunk to left.
> Count 3. Twist trunk to right.
> Count 4. Return to starting position.

Cadence: Moderate.

Category: **Thighs, Hips, Buttocks, Lower Back**

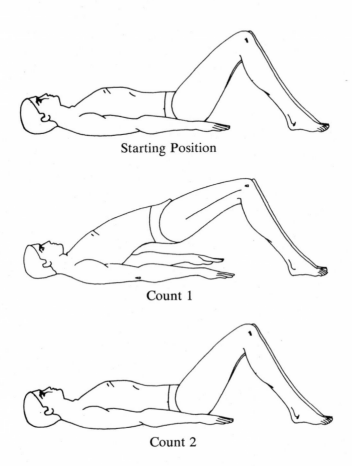

Starting Position

Count 1

Count 2

Hip Raise

Starting Position: Lie on back with knees bent in an angle of 45 to 90 degrees. Arms at sides with palms flat on floor.

Count 1. Raise hips off floor as high as possible, but keep shoulders and feet on floor. Tighten buttocks and abdominal muscles, and hold for a count of five seconds. Gradually increase hold count to ten.

Count 2. Return to starting position.

Cadence: Slow.

Category: **Arms, Shoulders, Chest**

Starting Position

Count 1

Count 2

Classic Push-up

Starting Position: With feet together squat down and place palms flat on floor. Hands should be about shoulder width apart and inside knees. Thrust legs backward into the front-leaning rest position, as in Starting Position illustration.

> Count 1. Keeping body and legs straight, bend elbows until chest touches floor.
> Count 2. By straightening arms, return to starting position.

Cadence: Moderate.

NOTE: If you are unable to do the classic push-up, then continue with modified push-ups as described in the beginning level.

MEN'S BASIC FIVE PROGRESSION CHART
(Maintenance Level — Four Weeks)

Week	Abdomen Isolated Curl				Trunk (Waist) Full Twister				Thighs, Hips, Buttocks, Lower Back Mountain Climber				Arms, Shoulders, Chest 8-Count Push-up				Cardiorespiratory System Walk/Run-in-Place or Skip Rope
	1st	2nd	3rd	4th	1st	2nd	3rd	4th	1st	2nd	3rd	4th	1st	2nd	3rd	4th	
Ages 18–29	14	16	18	20	10	12	14	16	14	17	20	24	10	12	14	16	Run 6 min. Increase stress by increasing speed. Skip rope 5 min. Increase speed.
Ages 30–39	10	12	14	16	8	10	12	14	12	14	16	20	8	10	12	14	Run 5 min. Increase stress by increasing speed. Skip rope 4 min. Increase to 5 min.
Ages 40–49	6	8	10	12	6	8	10	10	8	10	12	14	6	8	10	12	Run 4 min. Increase to 5 min. Skip rope 3 min. Increase to 4 min.
	Or continue bent-knee curls: 22 | 24 | 26 | 28																
Age 50 plus	Continue bent-knee half-curls: 14 | 15 | 16 | 16				4	6	8	8	6	8	9	10	Continue with modified push-ups: 10 | 11 | 12 | 12				Run 30 sec. Increase to 1 min.; walk 1 min. Repeat 3 times.

NOTE: Figures in boxes represent the number of repetitions.

MEN'S MAINTENANCE LEVEL
Category: **Abdomen**

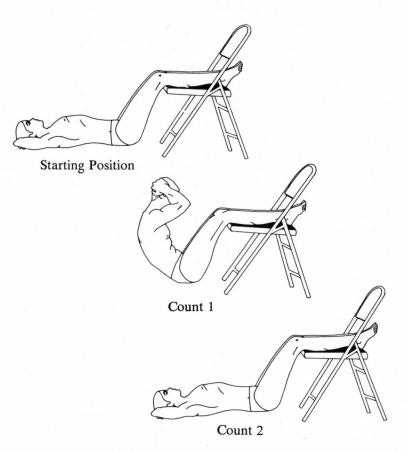

Starting Position

Count 1

Count 2

Isolated Curl

Starting Position: Lie on back, knees bent, feet resting on chair or sofa, hands interlaced behind head.

Action: Count 1. Tucking chin into chest, curl forward into sitting position and hold for count of three seconds.

Count 2. Return to starting position.

Cadence: Slow.

NOTE: If you can't do this exercise immediately, then build up to it by starting out with your arms extended over your head and swinging them forward as you sit up. Slide your hips away from chair to make exercise less difficult, closer to chair to make it more difficult.

Category: **Trunk (Waist)**

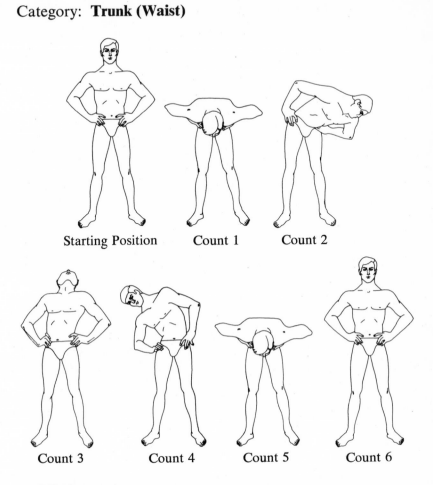

Starting Position   Count 1   Count 2

Count 3   Count 4   Count 5   Count 6

Full Twister

Starting Position: Stand with feet separated about shoulder width. Hands on hips.

Action: Count 1. Bend forward from waist as far as possible.

Count 2. Turning in a circular pattern from the waist, move the trunk to the left.

Count 3. Continue to circle in the same direction until you are bending backward from the waist.

Count 4. Continue circle to right side.

Count 5. Continue circle to Count 1 position.

Count 6. Return to starting position.

Cadence: Moderate.

Category: **Thighs, Hips, Buttocks, Lower Back**

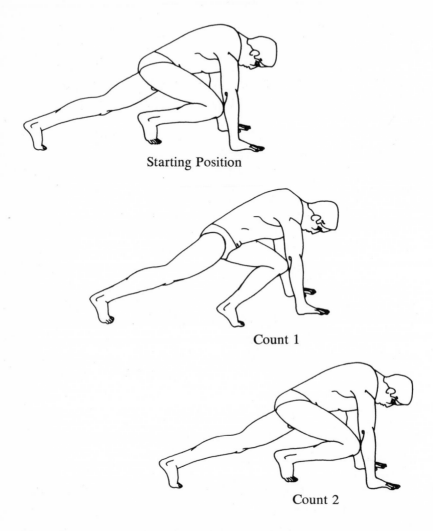

Starting Position

Count 1

Count 2

Mountain Climber

Starting Position: Squat with hands on floor. Left leg extended to rear. Right knee is inside right elbow.

Action: Count 1. Reverse position of feet simultaneously.
Count 2. Again reverse feet position, returning to starting position.

Cadence: Start at moderate pace. Switch to fast pace.

Category: **Arms, Shoulders, Chest**

Starting
Position

Count 1

Count 2

Count 3

Count 4

Count 5

Count 6

Count 7

Count 8

Eight-Count Push-up

Starting Position: Stand with feet together. Arms at sides. Head up.

Action: Count 1. Squat down. Place palms flat on floor about shoulder width apart. Arms inside knees.

Count 2. Thrust legs backward into front-leaning position, as in illustration.

Count 3. Bend arms, lowering body until chest touches floor.

Count 4. Raise to front-leaning position.

Count 5. Again touch chest to floor.

Count 6. Raise to front-leaning position.

Count 7. Return to squatting position.

Count 8. Return to starting position.

Cadence: Moderate.

WOMEN'S BASIC FIVE PROGRESSION CHART
(Beginning Level — Four Weeks)
Women 18-50 Plus

Week	Abdomen (Knee Draw)				Trunk (Waist) (Side Bend)				Thighs, Hips, Buttocks (Buttocks Contraction)	Arms, Shoulders, Chest (Arm Circles)				Cardiorespiratory System (Walk/Run-in-Place)
	1st	2nd	3rd	4th	1st	2nd	3rd	4th		1st	2nd	3rd	4th	
Ages 18–29	6	8	10	12	6	8	10	12	Hold 3 times for 6 sec.	Repeat 3 times				Run 1 min. Gradually increase to 2 min.
Ages 30–39	4	6	8	10	4	6	8	10	Hold 3 times for 6 sec.	2	2	3	3	Run ½ min. Gradually increase to 2 min.
Ages 40–49	4	4	6	8	4	4	6	6	Hold 3 times for 6 sec.	1	2	3	3	Run ¼ min. Gradually increase to 1 min. Walk 1 min.
Age 50 plus	3	3	4	5	2	3	4	4	Hold 3 times for 6 sec.	1	1	2	2	Walk in place 2 min.

NOTE: The number of repetitions (figures in the boxes) are based on exercising six days a week. If you exercise only three days a week, then allow twice the length of time at each level. For example, if the chart calls for you to do six repetitions each day but you go the three-day route, then do six repetitions every other day for two weeks before going on to the next level.

WOMEN'S BEGINNING LEVEL
Category: **Abdomen**

Starting Position

Count 1

Count 2

Count 3

Count 4

Knee Draw

Starting Position: Lie on back, arms extended out at the sides, palms against floor for support, legs straight, feet together.

Action: Count 1. Slowly draw knees back to chest, bringing heels as close to buttocks as possible while keeping knees and feet together.
              Count 2. Slowly stretch legs upward until they are straight and at right angles to the floor, with toes together and pointed at ceiling.
              Count 3. Slowly return to Count 1 position.
              Count 4. Slowly return to starting position.

Cadence: Slow.

Category: **Trunk (Waist)**

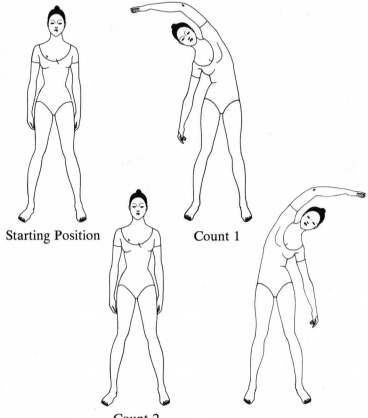

Starting Position

Count 1

Count 2

Side Bend

Starting Position: Stand erect, arms at sides, feet separated shoulder width. Keep legs straight.

Action: Count 1. Raise left arm sideward and over your head. With chest high, pelvis firm, and abdomen tucked in, bend your left arm and trunk to the right until you feel pull at your waist. Hold position for count of four seconds.
Count 2. Return to starting position.
Repeat with right side bend.

Cadence: Slow.

Category: **Thighs, Hips, Buttocks, Lower Back**

Starting Position

Buttocks Contraction

Starting Position: Lie on stomach, arms folded and chin resting
comfortably on hands. Legs straight, feet together, toes
pointed.

Action: Count 1. Contract muscles by firmly squeezing buttocks together. Tense and hold for a six-
second count.

Count 2. Relax for a six-second count.

Cadence: Slow.

Category: **Arms, Shoulders, Chest**

Count 1

Count 2

Arm Circles

Starting Position: Stand with feet separated shoulder width. Head up, buttocks and stomach tucked in. Arms extended out from shoulders parallel to floor.

Action: Count 1. With palms up, rotate arms backward 12 times. Begin with small circles, increasing the arc until by the 12th count you are rotating arms in largest possible circle.

            Count 2. Drop arms to side and relax.

            Repeat with forward rotation, palms of hands turned down.

Cadence: Moderate.

WOMEN'S BASIC FIVE PROGRESSION CHART
(Intermediate Level — Four Weeks)
Women 18-50

Week	Abdomen (Bent-Knee Curl)				Trunk (Waist) (Side Leg Lift)				Thighs, Hips, Buttocks, Lower Back (Kneeling Leg Lift)				Arms, Shoulders, Chest (Pectoralis Press)	Cardiorespiratory System (Walk/Run-in-Place)
	1st	2nd	3rd	4th	1st	2nd	3rd	4th	1st	2nd	3rd	4th		
Ages 18-29	10	12	14	16	6	8	10	12	8	10	12	14	Press 3 times, hold for 6 sec.	Run 2 min. Gradually increase to 4 min.
Ages 30-39	6	8	10	12	4	6	8	10	6	8	10	12	Press 3 times, hold for 6 sec.	Run 2 min. Gradually increase to 4 min.
Ages 40-49	4	4	6	8	Continue side bend 6	6	6	6	4	4	6	8	Press 3 times, hold for 6 sec.	Run 1 min. Increase to 2 min. Walk 2 min.
Age 50 plus	Continue knee draw 5	5	6	6	Continue side bend 4	4	4	5	3	3	4	4	Press 3 times, hold for 6 sec.	Walk in place 4 min.

NOTE: Figures in boxes represent number of repetitions.

WOMEN'S INTERMEDIATE LEVEL
Category: **Abdomen**

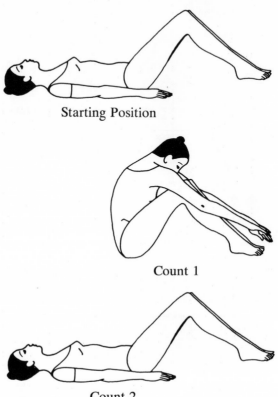

Starting Position

Count 1

Count 2

Bent-Knee Curl

Starting Position: Lie on back, arms at sides, legs together, knees bent at 45-degree angle, and feet firmly planted on floor.

Action: Count 1. Slowly curl forward, first tucking chin against your chest. Then continue curling your body forward until your head and shoulders are off the floor. Do not use either your arms or hands for support. Use your arms for balance only.

Count 2. Slowly uncurl to starting position.

Cadence: Slow.

Category: **Trunk (Waist)**

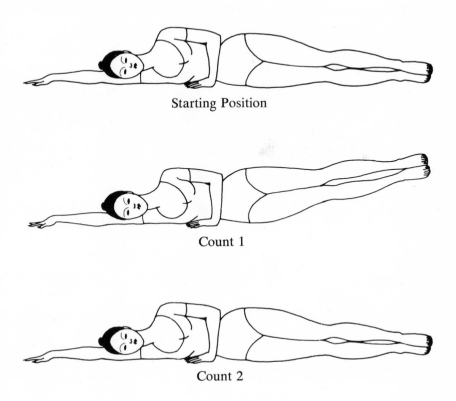

Starting Position

Count 1

Count 2

Side Leg Lift

Starting Position: Lie on right side with the body kept in a
straight line, right arm straight and extended under
your head. Place palm of left hand on floor alongside
your chest for support. Legs should be straight, one
on top of the other. Do not roll forward or backward
during the exercise.

Action: Count 1. Slowly raise both legs, keeping them together, until your feet are about 12 inches
off the floor. Hold for count of four seconds.
Count 2. Slowly return to starting position.
Repeat exercise on other side.

Cadence: Slow.

Category: **Thighs, Hips, Buttocks, Lower Back**

Starting Position

Count 1

Count 2
Count 3

Count 4

Count 5

Kneeling Leg Lift

Starting Position: Kneeling front rest: head up with weight evenly supported on both hands and both knees.

Action: Count 1. Extend left leg backward, toes pointed, leg straight.

Count 2. Raise leg until it is hip high and parallel to the floor.

Count 3. Hold leg in parallel position for four seconds.

Count 4. Lower leg slowly until toes touch floor.

Count 5. Return to starting position.

Repeat exercise with right leg.

Cadence: Slow.

Category: **Arms, Shoulders, Chest**

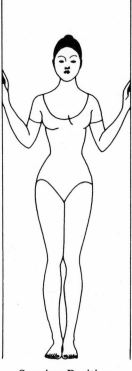

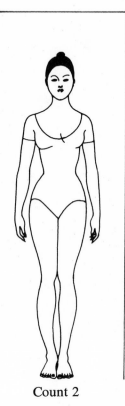

Starting Position
Count 1

Count 2

Pectoralis Press

Starting Position: Stand in frame of open doorway, feet together and palms against side of door frame at about height of your shoulders.

Action: Count 1. Press as hard as you can against the sides of the door frame, with chin and buttocks tucked in. Hold press for six seconds.

Count 2. Drop arms to side and relax.

Cadence: Slow.

WOMEN'S BASIC FIVE PROGRESSION CHART
(Maintenance Level — Four Weeks)
Ages 18-50 Plus

Week	Abdomen Elevated Curl-up				Trunk (Waist) Supine Leg Lift				Thighs, Hips, Buttocks, Lower Back Advanced Kneeling Leg Lift				Arms, Shoulders, Chest Modified Push-up				Cardiorespiratory System Walk/Run-in-Place
	1st	2nd	3rd	4th	1st	2nd	3rd	4th	1st	2nd	3rd	4th	1st	2nd	3rd	4th	
Ages 18–29	10	12	14	16	10	12	14	16	10	12	14	16	12	14	16	18	Run 5 min.
Ages 30–39	6	8	10	12	6	8	10	12	6	8	10	12	10	12	14	16	Run 4 min. Gradually increase to 5 min.
Ages 40–49	Continue bent-knee curl 8	8	10	10	4	6	8	8	6	6	8	8	6	8	10	12	Run 3 min. Walk 2 min.
Age 50 plus	Continue knee draw 6	6	8	8	Continue side bend 5	5	5	5	4	4	4	4	4	4	6	6	Walk in place 5 min.

NOTE: Figures in boxes represent number of repetitions.

WOMEN'S MAINTENANCE LEVEL
Category: **Abdomen**

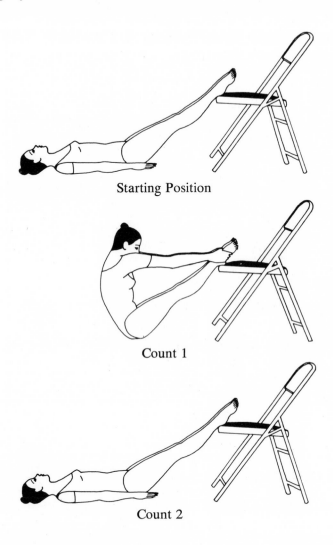

Starting Position

Count 1

Count 2

Elevated Curl-up

Starting Position: Lie on back, arms at sides. Elevate legs by placing heels on edge of chair or sofa.

Action: Count 1. Slowly curl forward, following directions for Bent-Knee Curl (page 38).

           Count 2. Slowly uncurl to starting position.

Cadence: Slow.

Category: **Trunk (Waist)**

Starting Position

Count 1

Count 2

Supine Leg Lift

Starting Position: Using your hands for support, sit on floor in back-leaning rest position: legs straight, feet together, toes pointed. Raise buttocks off floor until trunk and legs make a straight line supported only by hands and feet.

Action: Count 1. Raise right leg slowly, keeping body straight and toes pointed. Lift leg as high as possible.

Count 2. Lower right leg slowly.

Repeat with left leg.

Cadence: Slow.

Category: **Thighs, Hips, Buttocks, Lower Back**

Starting Position   Count 1

Count 2

Count 3

Count 4

Count 5   Count 6

Advanced Kneeling Leg Lift

Starting Position: Kneeling front rest: head up, weight evenly supported on both hands and both knees.

Action: Count 1. Extend left leg backward, toes pointed, leg straight.

Count 2. Raise leg until it is hip high and parallel to floor.

Count 3. Move leg laterally as far as you can to the left.

Count 4. Return to Count 2 position.

Count 5. Return to Count 1 position.

Count 6. Return to starting position.

Repeat exercise with right leg, moving leg laterally as far as you can to the right on Count 3.

Cadence: Slow.

Category: **Arms, Shoulders, Chest**

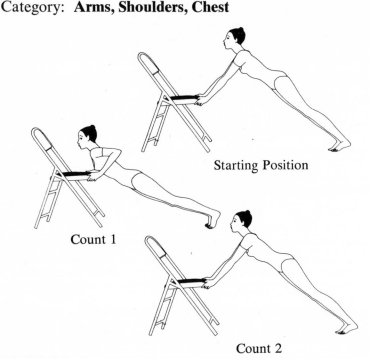

Starting Position

Count 1

Count 2

Modified Push-up

Starting Position: Place hands about shoulder width apart on front edge of bed (or sturdy chair or bench). Now move your feet backward until your legs and back are in a straight line, your body weight being supported only by your feet and your hands.

Action: Count 1. Keeping your head up, bend arms at elbows and lower your body until your chest touches front edge of bed.

Count 2. Push up, straightening arms until you have returned to starting position.

Cadence: Moderate.

NOTE: If this exercise is too easy, you can do push-ups off a hassock, stool, or for maximum stress, off the floor. If the exercise is too difficult, then push off a desk, table, kitchen counter, or for the least stress, the side of a wall. Understand that the higher your hands are placed, the less body weight you are lifting. For progressive conditioning of the upper torso, you literally work your way down to floor push-ups. When pushing off a chair, stool, bench, etc., place furniture against wall for added support and safety.

CHAPTER 3

The Walk/Run Plan

You're not going to have any trouble getting rid of that waistline bulge—the diet works, and a few minutes a day of exercise firms up abdominal muscles. So you're beautiful.

And if you want to hit that ball harder, a few light weight-lifting exercises in Chapter 10, BBC—Beyond Basic Conditioning, will take care of that. So now you're beautiful and playing a better game. All of this is ego gratifying but not pertinent to keeping you alive. All it guarantees is that you will be a beautiful corpse. What you've yet to do is begin to "run for your life."

In the past several years West Point has emphasized and re-emphasized its running program. Everyone is running—cadets, officers, and officers' wives and children, ranging in age from their teens into their middle fifties. No matter where a visitor stands, there appears to be a runner rising and falling on the horizon.

The running program for cadets begins on the first day they report. The object is to improve the efficiency of lungs, blood vessels and heart. The immediate pay-off is increased vigor, the ability to work efficiently under stress, and the capacity to stand up in case of shock or emergency. However, West Pointers are also running for their lives.

Heart attack continues to be the nation's major killer, accounting for about 670,000 deaths each year. Many thousands of these deaths occur among men and women in their most productive years. And these are men and women with responsible jobs, children still in school and obligations to fulfill. And that's why we run.

We know that one important step a person can take to help prevent a heart attack is to strengthen his cardiorespiratory system through moderate exercise. The most direct exercise is jog-

47

ging, running or vigorous walking. These exercises result in rhythmic tensing and relaxing of the large skeletal muscles, and this in turn aids and stimulates the flow of blood through the lungs, heart and vascular system.

Just as you strengthen muscles with moderate stress, you must also gradually stress the cardiorespiratory system to improve its efficiency. This can be accomplished by maintaining your heartbeat at 70 percent of the maximum heart rate for a period of five or more minutes by jogging or walking vigorously.

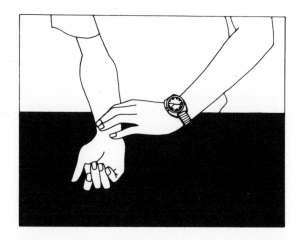

To monitor your heartbeat, merely take your pulse by placing the tips of one or two fingers on your radial artery, which is on the thumb side of your wrist. Count your pulse for ten seconds and multiply by six to get your heart rate for a minute.

Practice taking your pulse at rest, sitting quietly. Resting heart rates can vary from as low as 40 to as high as 100 and still fall within a normal range. However, for most healthy men the heart rate will be somewhere between 70 and 84 beats per minute, and for most healthy women, the rate will be between 75 and 85 beats per minute. If your heart rate doesn't fall within these ranges, you may, but not necessarily, require a medical examination.

To test your fitness for the following Walk/Run Plan, begin with a five-minute walk at a comfortable pace and immediately take your pulse because your heartbeat falls off rapidly once you stop exercising. Your pulse should be 50 percent of the maximum heart rate per minute for your age group (see the table on page 52).

Now walk vigorously for five minutes and again take your pulse, which should then be about 60 percent of maximum. If your heart is working at the 70-percent level for your age, you aren't in good condition. Continue taking vigorous five-minute walks on alternate days until your pulse falls below 70 percent.

The final test before starting the program is five minutes of slow jogging for one minute, alternating with one minute of vigorous walking. If your pulse rate stays below the 70-percent level, you may begin the Walk/Run Plan. If not, continue with five minutes of alternate running and walking every other day until you stay below 70 percent and then begin the plan.

The Walk/Run Plan itself also calls on you to alternate walking with running or jogging. The walking should always be vigorous, but the purpose of walking is to give you a breather, and during that time your pulse rate will fall below 70 percent of maximum. The object of jogging or running is to bring your pulse rate up to about 70 percent of maximum. If you are out of condition, you would most likely start out at a slow jog in the beginning level, and this is taken into consideration. You get much more time to cover a mile in the beginning level of the progression charts than you do by the time you've reached the maintenance level.

Another question concerns how long you run and how long you walk. At West Point, when new cadets begin the Walk/Run Plan, they alternate running six minutes and walking two. However, we have tested their conditioning and know that this pace is within their capability. How fast and long you run is also determined on the basis of your present conditioning, and that's why you have learned to take your pulse. You must get into the habit of testing yourself.

Run or jog for a minute at what you consider a comfortable pace. If your heart rate is between 60 and 70 percent, then you can continue running at that pace until you feel winded. Alternate with a vigorous walk for about one minute and then jog until you feel winded again. What will happen after several days is that you will get a "feel" of the pace. You won't have to check your wristwatch to see how long you have been walking or running. Then you will only have to check occasionally to make sure that you are working your heart at about 70 percent of maximum.

As your cardiorespiratory conditioning improves, you will

gradually have to increase your running pace to maintain about 70 percent of maximum, and this means you are getting results. In about four weeks you should have measurable results in a lower heart rate at rest. Generally, the lower your pulse, the healthier your cardiorespiratory system.

After completing the plan, continue at the maintenance level at least three alternate days a week to sustain cardiorespiratory health. Those who want to increase their endurance further may raise their pulse to 80 percent of maximum. Beyond 80 percent, the returns in conditioning are so small that it'd only be worthwhile for certain athletes such as marathon runners.

If you are in the 60-to-69-year-old age group and you have been running regularly, then keep it up. If you haven't, walk only. If you want to work up to a running schedule, begin with brisk walking for the first 12 weeks.

Some Questions About the Walk/Run Plan

Q. *Should I wear a sweat suit when jogging?*

A. You should not wear a sweat suit of material that will induce sweating. See Chapter 12, Tips for Better Performance, which includes specific information on choosing clothing and shoes, as well as tips on correct running and breathing.

Q. *Will running replace any of the other exercises in the Basic Five?*

A. No. Running does little, if anything, for the primary muscles in the torso and arms.

Q. *Are there any substitutes for running?*

A. Swimming, bicycling, and rope jumping are good substitutes. All you have to do is check your pulse to see if you are going about it vigorously enough.

Only your pulse rate will tell you if you're working at 70 percent of your maximum rate. A person in poor condition may reach 70 percent by merely walking fast. On the other hand, a person in good condition may not get up to 70 percent if he's jogging slowly, and therefore he would get no benefit out of jogging.

So whatever form of exercise you use, check your pulse rate to make sure that you're not wasting your time. How long you keep your pulse at that rate depends on your level in the progression chart. Use the same "minutes" recommendation in the substitute exercise.

Q. *Is there any way of dealing with the monotony?*

A. Once you've established the proper pace, you can let your mind roam and do some serious or fanciful thinking. You can carry a small radio in your pocket and listen to news or music. And if you have a treadmill or stationary bicycle, work out in front of your TV. If a six-day schedule is more than you can handle, it's strongly recommended that you immediately cut back to three alternate days a week. That is preferable to stopping completely.

Q. *How long can you take a "vacation" from the Walk/Run program before it becomes critical?*

A. Physiologists estimate that you begin to lose conditioning within 72 hours. Of course, if you stop completely, you lose it all, and so all of the work has been for nothing. Like muscular conditioning, cardiorespiratory conditioning cannot be stored.

Q. *Can I substitute tennis for the Walk/Run Plan?*

A. Not on a one-to-one basis. For three days of Walk/Run you'd have to substitute five or six days of vigorous tennis with at least one-hour workouts.

Q. *Why is the Walk/Run Plan different for men and women?*

A. Women don't have to work as hard to get their heart rate up to 70 percent because of physiological differences, including a smaller heart, lower hemoglobin count, and smaller lung capacity.

Q. *What's the best time of day to run?*

A. Any time is good except within an hour after meals. Early morning or evening is recommended because you can avoid the hot sun and also avoid traffic and traffic fumes if you live in a city.

Q. *If I have a low resting pulse rate does that mean I am physically fit?*

A. Not necessarily. There is a great variation in resting pulse rates. Within the same age group the rate can vary from 40 to over 90 beats per minute. You may have a lower than normal, or average, resting pulse but without CR conditioning you can be certain that you *are not* physically fit. If you haven't been running and begin now, your heart rate will decrease.

Q. *What is the meaning of maximum heart rate and how can I determine what mine is?*

A. Maximum heart rate is the fastest that your heart will beat during exercise. The maximum heart rate is affected by age—the older one gets, the lower the maximum heart rate. An estimate of your M.H.R. is: 220 beats per minute minus your age.

Q. *Is there any danger that I may exercise so hard that my heart rate will approach the maximum level?*

A. There is no danger if your heart is healthy. It's generally accepted that you cannot hurt a healthy heart. However, before beginning a program that might cause you to work at such a high level, especially if you aren't used to heavy work, you should visit your physician. If your doctor isn't equipped to monitor your heart with an exercise electrocardiogram while you work on a stepping bench, a treadmill or a bicycle ergometer, then you should see a cardiologist.

Q. *How will I know if I'm making progress?*

A. You'll know in many ways. You'll find yourself running to catch a bus, train, or a roving toddler with less exertion, and then you'll find your heart returning to normal more quickly once you stop running. You'll literally feel better and more vigorous. And if you wish a better test, turn to Chapter 5, Testing and Recording Your Progress where you will learn how to test and record your progress in various aspects of physical fitness.

ESTIMATED HEART RATES PER MINUTE FOR AVERAGE MAN OR WOMAN BY AGE GROUP

Age Group	Maximum Heart Rate	Exercise Level			
		80% Maximum Heart Rate	70% Maximum Heart Rate	60% Maximum Heart Rate	50% Maximum Heart Rate
18–29	203–191	162–153	142–134	112–144	101–95
30–39	190–181	152–145	133–127	113–108	95–90
40–49	180–171	144–137	126–120	107–102	90–85
50–59	170–161	136–129	119–113	101–96	85–80
60–69	160–151	128–121	112–106	95–90	80–75
70–79	150–141	120–113	105–99	89–94	75–70

THE WALK/RUN PROGRESSION CHART FOR MEN

Week	Beginning Level				Intermediate Level				Maintenance Level			
	1st	2nd	3rd	4th	1st	2nd	3rd	4th	1st	2nd	3rd	4th
Ages 18–29 Miles	1	1	1	1½	1½	1½	1½	2	2	2	2	2
Minutes	12	11	10	16	15	14	13	19	18	17	16	15
Ages 30–39 Miles	1	1	1	1	1½	1½	1½	1½	1½	2	2	2
Minutes	13	12	11	11	17½	16½	15½	14½	14	20½	19½	18½
Ages 40–49 Miles	1	1	1	1	1	1½	1½	1½	1½	1½	2	2
Minutes	15	14	13	12	12	19	18	16	15	14½	21½	20½
Ages 50–59 Miles	1	1	1	1	1	1	1½	1½	1½	1½	1½	2
Minutes	17	16	15	14	13	13	20½	19½	18½	17½	17	24
Ages 60–69[a] Miles	½	½	¾	¾	1	1	1½	1½	1½	2	2	2
Minutes	10	10	18	17	23	21	31	30	29	38	37	36

NOTE: Upper figure in each box represents *distance in miles*. Lower figure represents *number of minutes to run*. Example: First week, age 18–29: Keep alternately running and walking for a total of one mile in 12 minutes.

[a] Walk only.

THE WALK/RUN PROGRESSION CHART FOR WOMEN

	Week	Beginning Level				Intermediate Level				Maintenance Level			
		1st	2nd	3rd	4th	1st	2nd	3rd	4th	1st	2nd	3rd	4th
Ages 18–29	Miles	1	1	1	1½	1½	1½	1½	2	2	2	2	2
	Minutes	15	14	13	20	19	18	16	21	20	19	18	18
Ages 30–39	Miles	1	1	1	1	1	1½	1½	1½	1½	2	2	2
	Minutes	16	15	15	14	13	21	20	19	18	25	24	24
Ages 40–49	Miles	1	1	1	1	1	1	1½	1½	1½	1½	2	2
	Minutes	18	17	17	16	15	14	23	22	21	20	28	27
Ages 50–59	Miles	1	1	1	1	1	1	1	1½	1½	1½	1½	2
	Minutes	20	19	19	18	17	16	15	25	24	23	22	30
Ages 60–69[a]	Miles	½	½	¾	¾	1	1	1	1½	1½	1½	2	2
	Minutes	12	12	20	19	35	23	21	32	31	29	38	37

NOTE: Upper figure in each box represents *distance in miles.* Lower figure represents *number of minutes to run.* Example: First week, age 18–29: Keep alternately running and walking for a total of one mile in 15 minutes.

[a] Walk only.

CHAPTER 4

Flexibility: Tests and Exercises

Although all cadets are young and all pass a physical-aptitude examination, every one is tested individually for flexibility upon reporting to West Point. This underscores the following important points:

Flexibility may be a problem at any age—for the six-year-old, the ninety-year-old, and everyone in between. And for both the young and old poor flexibility not only limits physical activity but also results in injuries, muscular pain, and postural problems. For these reasons flexibility is considered a major component in physical fitness, and a particular problem for Americans.

A study comparing European and American children in the six-to-twelve-year-old range found that American children have a much larger number of failures in performing flexibility tests than youngsters from Austria, Switzerland, and Italy. The study concluded that the major cause is our sedentary way of life. We are mechanized and automated. We ride instead of walk, sit instead of stand.

The loss of flexibility begins in elementary school, when our children begin to spend a significant part of the day in a fixed position. Few schools have a physical education program that compensates for the sedentary life, and since the body follows the law of use and disuse, muscles begin to lose elasticity with inactivity. By the time the child is a young adult, poor flexibility may be the cause of accidents, fatigue, backache, and indirectly, headaches. Unfortunately, most people don't realize that they are the victims of decreased flexibility because the loss comes on so gradually. That's one problem. Another problem may be that many people don't know what flexibility is all about.

Defining Flexibility

There's a problem in understanding flexibility. Flexibility means one thing; the cause is something else. Flexibility, itself, refers only to the extent that you can move a joint through a normal range of motion. That includes bending, stretching, twisting and turning, lifting and throwing, pushing and pointing. All of this has to do with action at the joints, but flexibility is not usually dependent on the bony structure.

Most flexibility problems are caused by the connective tissue around the bone joint, including the muscles, tendons, and ligaments. It's the elasticity and length of these tissues that result in either good motion or the stiffness and clumsiness that occur when we concentrate on one sport or develop poor postural habits or even wear the wrong kind of shoes. Some examples:

You may have sore Achilles' tendons when you get out of bed in the morning, or you may learn about this soreness when you put on low shoes for the Walk/Run Plan. The cause is shortening of these tendons, which is common among people who wear high-heeled shoes. The tendons shorten to conform to the high heel, but then when you walk barefoot or wear sneakers or slippers, the tendons are strained.

Another problem occurs if you bend over a desk most of the day. Your back muscles stretch, and your chest muscles shorten. At first you become a little round shouldered. However, this can be progressive. At its worst the problem is known as a "dowager's hump."

Long periods of sitting are also responsible for the shortening of the hamstring muscles, which are on the back side of the thighs. Tight hamstrings are identified as the major cause of over 80 percent of lower-back pain, a very common ailment, which begins as early as age 25. What literally happens is that shortened hamstrings tilt the pelvis forward which in turn pushes the vertebrae in the lower-back region out of line, resulting in lower-back pain.

Shortened hamstring muscles are also responsible for "snapped muscles" that trouble both professional athletes and kids playing in sandlots, and the "pulled muscle" that unexpectedly hits a man sprinting for a bus or a woman reaching over to pick up a child.

Ridding yourself of pain and preventing injuries are reasons enough to be concerned about flexibility, but there are other rewards. Good flexibility contributes to good posture and a good game whatever your sport.

Testing Your Flexibility

The goal in flexibility is just enough—not too much and not too little. When you have too much flexibility, it means the musculature around the joints is not strong enough which may result in joint injuries such as dislocations or torn cartilage, tendons, or ligaments. Too much flexibility is generally only a problem for the very young, but it is a good enough reason to keep youngsters from playing in contact sports before they are tested for flexibility.

Only a physician has the equipment to test accurately for excessive flexibility, but the most common problem, the loss of flexibility, can be tested in the home, and these tests are included in the flexibility program.

Some Questions About Flexibility

Q. *How much time do you have to put into flexibility conditioning?*

A. The exercises are simple and literally take only a few minutes. Total time for all of them should be about four or five minutes.

Q. *Should you do the exercises at any special time?*

A. The first recommendation would be after you've warmed up your muscles with the Basic Five, but you can do them at the office or in front of television when you get up to stretch. And without sweat.

Q. *Are the tests different for children and adults?*

A. The tests are the same for all ages. The exercises are also the same for all ages except for those in the "later years." For the oldest age group, flexibility therapy is built into their Basic Six (see Chapter 9, The Later Years).

Q. *How long will it take to get results?*

A. If your flexibility is very poor, it will take a while. This in itself is a strong argument for maintaining flexibility with regular exercise.

Q. *How will I know if I'm making any headway if it takes so long to get results?*

A. The results are continuous but very gradual, a tiny fraction of an inch in a week, which makes progress difficult to measure in the home. So what you must be concerned with is doing the exercises properly. One measure of effectiveness is pain. In each of the exercises you must stretch until you feel an ache in the muscles being stressed and then hold that ache for the prescribed count. However, it is not an excruciating pain that will make you want to scream or cry, but it will be uncomfortable for two or three seconds. Once you have reached a good flexibility level, it won't hurt.

Q. *Can you injure yourself doing these exercises?*

A. Not if you go about doing them carefully and deliberately. Often you get the impression in films or television that when people do flexibility exercises, they are bouncing their bodies as they stretch toward the floor or a wall. That's wrong. That defeats the object of stretching the muscle carefully. By bobbing and bouncing, you may keep the muscles from relaxing enough to stretch. The proper method is a slow and gradual stretch, then hold.

Flexibility Tests and Exercises

The following tests will determine the level of flexibility of your lower back, hamstrings (back of thighs) and Achilles' tendons (heel cords). Two of the tests you will discover also serve as exercises. All the exercises are simple, including the alternates. The purpose of exercise is explained so that you can plan a flexibility program to meet your individual needs.

Category: **Lower-Back and Hamstring Muscles**

| Starting Position | Count 1 | Count 2 |

Seated Toe Touch (Test and Exercise)

Purpose: (1) To check the flexibility of the muscles of the lower back and the hamstring muscles.

(2) As an exercise to improve flexibility.

Starting Position: Sit on floor with feet against the wall, bookcase, or any heavy furniture. Keep legs straight with knees locked throughout the stretching period. Start with hands resting on the knees.

Action: Count 1. Bend forward slowly with arms straight and attempt to touch the wall with your fingertips. When you have bent forward as far as you can, you will feel the stretch stress in the muscles on the back of the thighs. Hold in this position for a count of five.

Count 2. Sit back and return to the starting position. Relax for a count of three and repeat.

Cadence: Perform the stretching slowly. Do not bounce or jerk into position.

Test: If your fingertips come within four inches of the wall, your flexibility of the low back and hamstring muscles is only satisfactory. A sign of good flexibility is being able to touch the wall with your fingertips.

Exercise Progression: Perform three repetitions two times each day for the first week. After the first week increase gradually to five repetitions and increase holding period to ten seconds each time. The exercise should be done five days a week when you are improving your flexibility. For maintenance do the exercise three days a week.

Category: **Lower Back**

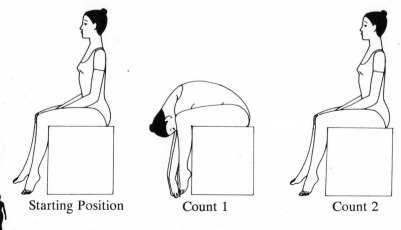

Starting Position   Count 1   Count 2

Seated Curl (Test and Exercise)

Purpose: To test and exercise the flexibility of the lower back.

Starting Position: Sit on a table or desk with lower legs hanging over the edge. Sit back so that the edge of the tabletop is supporting the knee joints. Knees should be slightly separated.

Action: Count 1. Tuck chin into your chest and slowly curl forward, trying to lower your forehead between your knees. Continue to stretch until you feel the stress in the lower back. Hold for a count of five seconds.

Count 2. Return to the starting position and relax for three seconds.

Cadence: Perform slowly. Do not bounce into position.

Test: If your forehead only touches your knees, your lower-back flexibility is only satisfactory. Good flexibility is present when you lower your head all the way between your knees.

Exercise Progression: Perform three repetitions two times each day for the first week. After the first week increase gradually to five repetitions and increase holding period to ten seconds each time. The exercise should be done a minimum of five days a week when you are improving your flexibility. For maintenance do the exercise three days a week.

Category: **Achilles' Tendons (Heel Cords)**

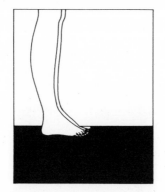

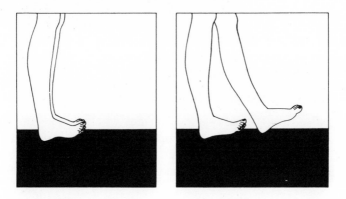

Heel Walk (Test)

Purpose: To test the flexibility of the Achilles' tendons.

Starting Position: In bare feet or wearing soft-heeled shoes, balance yourself on your heels by raising your toes off the floor.

Action: Walk ten steps on your heels only.

Cadence: Moderate Pace.

Test: If you can maintain your balance while walking ten steps on your heels, then the flexibility of your Achilles' tendons is satisfactory.

NOTE: This is only a test. See "Achilles'-Tendon Stretcher," page 62 for exercise.

Category: **Achilles' Tendons (Heel Cords)**

Starting Position

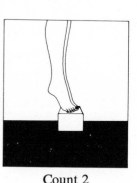

Count 1

Count 2

Achilles'-Tendon Stretcher (Exercise)

Purpose: To stretch the Achilles' tendons and calf muscles.

Starting Position: Stand with your toes on the edge of a step (or three- to four-inch-high board, brick, etc.). Your heels will protrude over the edge.

Action: Count 1. Lower your heels to a level below your toes until you feel the stretch stress in the Achilles' tendons and calf muscles. Hold for a count of five seconds.

Count 2. Return to starting position, with the heels and toes at the same level.

Cadence: Stretch slowly and carefully.

Exercise Progression: Perform three repetitions two times each day for the first week. After the first week increase gradually to five repetitions and increase holding period to ten seconds each time. The exercise should be done a minimum of five days a week when you are improving your flexibility. For maintenance do the exercise three days a week.

NOTE: If during the first few days of exercise your heel cords become too sore, reduce the hold time to a count of three and then increase gradually.

ALTERNATE EXERCISES
Category: **Hamstring Muscles**

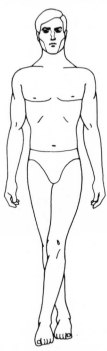

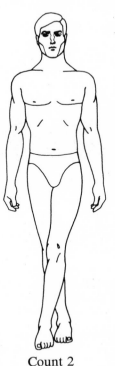

| Starting Position | Count 1 | Count 2 |

Crossed-Legs Stretch

Purpose: To stretch the hamstring muscles—the muscles on the back side of the thighs.

Starting Position: Stand and cross your legs with one leg in front of the other.

Action: Count 1. Bend slowly from the waist and try to touch the floor in front of your toes. Reach until you feel the stretch stress in the back side of the thigh of the back leg. Hold the lowest position for a count of five seconds.

Count 2. Return to the starting position. Relax for a count of three. (Switch position of the legs and repeat the exercise.)

Cadence: Stretch slowly. Do not bounce.

Exercise Progression: Same as the Seated Toe Touch (page 59).

Category: **Lower Back**

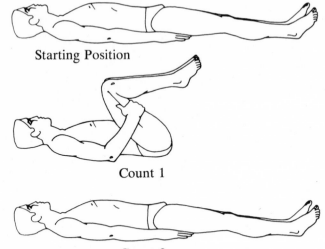

Starting Position

Count 1

Count 2

Knee-to-Chest Pull

Purpose: To stretch the muscles of the lower back.

Starting Position: Lie on your back with legs extended, straight and together.

Action: Count 1. Bring both knees to your chest, grasping your legs with your hands just under the knees. Pull your knees toward your shoulders until you feel stretch stress in the muscles of your lower back. Hold for a count of five seconds.

Count 2. Return to the starting position and relax for a count of three seconds.

Cadence: Stretch slowly and carefully.

Exercise Progression: Same as the Seated Toe Touch (page 59).

NOTE 1: If you are already suffering from severe lower-back pain, see your physician. Take along this manual and ask him if he recommends any exercises in addition to those described.

NOTE 2: The satisfactory and good levels of flexibility described here are true for *most* people but not necessarily all because people are genetically different. If you are in doubt, ask your doctor for individual guidance.

CHAPTER 5

Weight Control and Nutrition

Some myths we perpetuate are self-serving. One such is that slimming down is of concern only to skinny models, people who preen, or those who are obsessed with appearance. In fact obesity is as much a danger to your health as smoking, inactivity, or disease.

Another self-serving myth is that physical activity alone is an effective way of working off excess fat. The executive walks to the office to lose a bulging midriff, but the bulge doesn't go away. The overweight housewife tells you that she puts in a lot of hard work in the home—and she does—but the fat stays on. And now hear this about West Point cadets:

It's unlikely that any other student body in the country works at the same level of physical intensity as the cadets. They exercise, parade, run, participate in intramural sports, hike, take combat training—and yet, despite a rigorous physical program, some cadets put on excess fat.

There's an absolute need for proper exercise, and exercise can work off some calories, but most of us have an exaggerated idea about the number of calories (energy or fat) that we burn up in ordinary activities. Keeping in mind that you must use *3,600 calories* to lose one pound, consider the following:

For a 150-pound person, the energy expenditure in one hour of
Bicycling at 5.5 mph: 300 calories
Horseback riding, walk: 98 calories
Horseback riding, trot: 301 calories
Ice skating: 245 calories
Running 5.5 mph (11 min./mile): 648 calories
Swimming 2 mph: 553 calories

And in the home:
    Dishwashing: 70 calories
    Ironing with a five-pound iron: 70 calories
    Painting furniture: 105 calories
    Paring potatoes: 42 calories
    Washing floors: 84 calories

Translating these figures into actual work means that if you rely only on physical activity, you would have to wash floors for nearly 43 hours to drop one pound, or if you prefer, chop wood for about 8 hours. All of this simply means that although we need moderate exercise for health, we must establish intelligent eating habits to control body weight.

Back to the Basic Truth

There's nothing complicated about understanding how to control weight. The diet fads and gimmicks we are so often exposed to tend to obscure this simple truth: Protein, carbohydrates, and fat all contain calories; if we take in more calories than our body can use, the excess calories are stored as fat. To lose weight, we must ingest fewer calories than the body normally requires so that our body will burn up the calories (fat) in storage. When we have reached a desirable weight, we maintain that weight by consuming the same number of calories that our body uses.

There's another basic truth about dieting that is just as important, and that concerns nutrition. Whatever our motivation in dieting, our body cannot maintain health without a proper balance of nutrients, which includes many different minerals, vitamins, fats, proteins, and carbohydrates. And that is another reason why West Point doesn't believe in medically unsound fad and crash diets. Instead, the West Point Diet provides all nutrients in adequate amounts. However, calories will be limited. This will result in your burning up excess fat now stored in unsightly flaps and rolls.

Obesity—A Self-inflicted Illness

Fat is bad only in excess. In fact, fat is necessary as an insulator for the maintenance of body heat and temperature and, also, for protecting and keeping body organs in proper position.

However, beyond this basic level, fat becomes dead weight and is deadly. Generally, 15 percent of body weight is considered a normal limit of body fat for men, and 22 percent is considered normal for women. (The extra percentage for women is accounted for by subcutaneous fat, which is a distinct sexual difference.) At West Point a male cadet with 20 percent or more body fat is considered obese, a woman with 25 percent or more. A cadet may be expelled for obesity because obesity is considered a loss of physical fitness.

Obesity is a self-inflicted illness, almost always caused by overeating, and some physicians consider overeating a kind of suicide. Overweight people have a greater tendency to develop a number of serious diseases, including diabetes, gallstones, arthritis, hypertension, and cardiorespiratory ailments. Even in ordinary daily activities obese people have to work almost twice as hard to merely breathe. These are some of the reasons that we are so serious about weight control at West Point.

The Inch Pinch Test

If you want a scientific estimate of your excess body fat, you must see a physician or technician who is experienced in the use of calipers to measure folds of fat. However, if you stand naked in front of a mirror, you can make a rough assessment yourself. Look for folds of fat around the stomach and waistline. Below the hip bones look for "saddlebags" and above the hips for "love handles." Take a side view of your buttocks and see if they droop with fat. Tighten the muscles in your legs; the flesh that doesn't tighten up is fat.

Instead of calipers you can use your thumb and index fingers to pinch for fat. For example, raise your arm to see if fat dangles from the back of your upper arm. If you can pinch more than three quarters of an inch of fat, that's an indication of obesity. In other areas where a full inch pinch tells you that you're in the obese range are (1) your waistline just to the right or left of your navel, (2) the front of your thigh about halfway to your knee, (3) your chest halfway between your left nipple and your shoulder.

Another way of checking for obesity is the girth test which is explained in the following chapter, Testing and Recording Your Progress, which provides recommended girth proportions for men and women: the chest compared to the waist, the hips, thighs, calves, and ankles.

Setting a Goal

Both the mirror and tape measure will tell you a lot about your health and appearance, but once you've decided to diet, you should have a concrete goal. You may ask your physician how much weight you should lose when you get permission to diet. Or you may refer to the Desirable Weights tables on page 69, which are generally accepted by dieticians and physicians and are based on studies that corrolate weight to life-span.

If the weights appear to be a little low, it's because people who live the longest weigh less than the average person. If the recommended weight sounds faintly familiar, it's because the figure is probably what you weighed in your early twenties. When Dr. Paul Dudley White, the eminent cardiologist, was living, he spoke at West Point annually, and his challenge to cadets was this: "If you are in good physical condition when you are twenty-one years old, then you should never weigh more than you do at that age."

You can also use these tables to roughly determine if you are either overweight or obese. If you weigh 10 percent more than is desirable, that's overweight; 20 percent more is obese. But, the tables are not foolproof. A weightlifter, for example, could be overweight but not obese. On the other hand, a sedentary person may have obese folds of fat without being excessively overweight. Therefore, use your bathroom mirror, scales, and pinch test for a final determination.

How the West Point Diet Works

A 1,200-calorie diet is usually prescribed for obese cadets and other adults at the Academy because they will lose fat at what is considered a medically sound rate—about one or two pounds a week. Exactly how much weight you lose per week depends on several factors.

On a daily 1,200-calorie diet you should lose excess fat at the rate of about 1 percent of your total body weight each week. This means a 200-pound person would lose about two pounds; a 150-pound person, about a pound and a half. Another factor is

DESIRABLE WEIGHTS
Men of Ages 25 and Over
Weight in Pounds According to Frame (In Indoor Clothing)

HEIGHT (with shoes on) 1-inch heels Feet Inches	SMALL FRAME	MEDIUM FRAME	LARGE FRAME
5 2	112–120	118–129	126–141
5 3	115–123	121–133	129–144
5 4	118–126	124–136	132–148
5 5	121–129	127–139	135–152
5 6	124–133	130–143	138–156
5 7	128–137	134–147	142–161
5 8	132–141	138–152	147–166
5 9	136–145	142–156	151–170
5 10	140–150	146–160	155–174
5 11	144–154	150–165	159–179
6 0	148–158	154–170	164–184
6 1	152–162	158–175	168–189
6 2	156–167	162–180	173–194
6 3	160–171	167–185	178–199
6 4	164–175	172–190	182–204

Women of Ages 25 and Over

HEIGHT (with shoes on) 2-inch heels Feet Inches	SMALL FRAME	MEDIUM FRAME	LARGE FRAME
4 10	92– 98	96–107	104–119
4 11	94–101	98–110	106–122
5 0	96–104	101–113	109–125
5 1	99–107	104–116	112–128
5 2	102–110	107–119	115–131
5 3	105–113	110–122	118–134
5 4	108–116	113–126	121–138
5 5	111–119	116–130	125–142
5 6	114–123	120–135	129–146
5 7	118–127	124–139	133–150
5 8	122–131	128–143	137–154
5 9	126–135	132–147	141–158
5 10	130–140	136–151	145–163
5 11	134–144	140–155	149–168
6 0	138–148	144–159	153–173

For young women between 18 and 25, subtract 1 pound for each year under 25. By permission of Metropolitan Life Insurance Company.

NOTE: The absence of a similar measurement rule for young men between 18 and 25 is explained in part by the difference in growth periods for the sexes. Young women don't grow much taller after age 16 and add little weight after the age of 18, except for unwanted fat. On the other hand, the growth period of young men may continue into their early twenties.

sex. The metabolism of men is generally 10 percent higher than women's, and so men will lose a little faster on the same diet at the same level of activity. The third factor is age. The metabolism of both sexes goes into a very gradual decrease after the age of 20; so the older you are, the less rapidly you will lose fat.

If you want to lose weight quickly, then you should check into a hospital or sanitarium, since anyone choosing to lose more than two pounds a week should have constant and close medical supervision. The virtue of the West Point 1,200-calorie diet is that you still have balanced nutrition, which is to say enough carbohydrates, fats, proteins, vitamins, minerals, and water for energy as well as repair and maintenance of your body. You will be shorted only in the number of calories ingested; as a result, you will begin to use up some of your body fat during normal metabolism.

And You Don't Have to Count and Count

The diet is based on the Food-Exchange System. Among the foods listed, you'll find those that you have always enjoyed with your family and friends—which means you'll be spared the inconvenience and expense of making up special dishes for yourself. Generally you will only be modifying the amounts of food rather than the kinds that you eat, for there are just a few foods that are forbidden.

The diet works on the simple portion principle. In most cases you will need only a cup, tablespoon, or teaspoon to measure your food allowance. In the beginning you may have to weigh a portion of meat, but after a little experience your eye will be able to identify a medium-size chicken breast or two, small well-trimmed chops as examples of three-ounce portions, or if you divide a pound of hamburger into four patties, each will be about three ounces by the time it is broiled.

Why Is It Called an Exchange System?

There are six different food categories: bread, fat, fruit, meat, milk, and vegetables. Each of these categories has a separate exchange list. For example, in the Fruit-Exchange List, you will find 70 different kinds of fruits, each with a designated portion size. Each of the 70 has virtually the same nutritional values—that is, the same amount of carbohydrate, fat, protein, and calories. This means you can exchange any food on the list for another on the list without the nagging fear that you may be going off your diet.

You will be told exactly how many fruit, meat, bread, fat, milk, and vegetable exchanges you are allowed for a whole day. The diet will suggest how you should allot the exchanges by meals, but, just as in the exercise program, you may tailor the exchanges to your own needs. Instead of three meals a day you may have four, five, or six, just as long as you don't exceed the total number of exchanges allowed for one day.

Also, the Food-Exchange System gives you the freedom of planning meals to the tastes of yourself and your friends and family. Usually, diets list specific foods for each meal, recipes for preparing the dish, and complete menus by the day, week, or month. This has put off many people in a nation where there are so many different ethnic and regional tastes in foods. Instead of being told what to serve, you make your own choice from the exchange lists, and you can further modify the food for special tastes.

A Maintenance Diet

After you have reached your desired weight, you can compute a maintenance diet by multiplying your ideal or desirable weight by 15. For example, this would be 1,650 calories per day for a 110-pound person up to the age of 25. From the age of 25 on, as metabolism decreases, you should cut down on caloric intake. From 25 to 35 years, reduce calories by 3 percent; from 35 to 45, by 5 percent; 45 to 55, by 9 percent; 55 to 65, by 13 percent; and over 65, by 17 percent.

If your maintenance diet allows you to go over 1,200 calories per day, increase your food intake gradually. Begin by allowing yourself an additional 200 calories per week, and at the end of the week check with your scales. There are individual differences in metabolism and physical activity that you must take into account and monitor. Caution and concentration are the watchwords when you increase caloric intake.

Some Questions Asked About the Weight-Control Plan

Q. *Without recommended menus how can I be sure that my nutrition will be balanced over long periods of time?*

A. The answer is to vary your foods from meal to meal and from day to day. One day it may be beef; and the next, chicken; and the next, fish; and the next, ham. Also vary your vegetables and fruits. No one food by itself has all the nutrients needed for health, growth, and body maintenance.

Another way to ensure variety is to break away from fixed eating patterns. You don't have to have a citrus fruit for breakfast every morning if during the day you have a fruit or vegetable that contains vitamin C. You can have grits for dinner and your potato in the morning. You can have a toasted cheese sandwich, enchilada, or even a lamb chop for breakfast and your egg at lunch. It's only important that your nutrition balance out for the day and the week.

Q. *Can you put an obese child on a 1,200-calorie diet?*

A. First consult a physician. A physician or the school nurse might readily prescribe a 1,200-calorie diet, but the decision should be based on the individual child. Growth periods differ, and the amount of physical activity varies from child to child. It is important to be seriously concerned about an obese child. Studies have found that extremely overweight children continue to be overweight as adults. Besides considering a diet for the child, be sure the child is getting enough exercise, because more daily activity may be all the child needs to control weight.

Q. *Is weight reduction always desirable?*

A. No. Not for people under emotional stress. Not when people are using certain medications. Not if you are already at a desirable weight and have an obsession with being obsessively thin. There are other reasons, and that's why we recommend that you check with your physician before starting an exercise plan and diet.

Q. *Can you ever go off the maintenance diet?*

A. Yes, eventually something very nice will happen. In the beginning, if you have been overeating, you will have to break a bad habit. Your body won't complain too much because a 1,200-calorie diet is nutritionally balanced. Before too long you will suddenly discover you are eating moderate quantities of food without thinking about the discipline involved. You will have developed a new habit of eating, and at the same time you will have learned to balance your nutrition.

Q. *How often should I weigh myself?*

A. Once a week is enough. See the following chapter, Testing and Recording Your Progress, for some special tips on how to maintain accuracy.

Q. *How do I account for calories when I eat processed or frozen foods?*

A. Use one of the paperback books that lists nutritional information for brand foods. Or, if you favor a particular brand of canned foods, write the company and ask for nutritional information on its products. Also, read the ingredient information on the package: Ingredients are always listed in order according to quantity.

Q. *Can I get rid of a thick waistline with abdominal exercises instead of dieting?*

A. Your abdominal muscles will become firmer when you exercise, but you can't expect to lose a significant amount of fat from your waistline. Exercise burns fat from all over the body. Similarly, fat loss in dieting is general rather than from specific areas.

Q. *Don't you ever recommend exercise to lose excess fat?*

A. Exercise is an excellent aid in controlling body weight. For example, regular, vigorous exercise will dispose of fat: Four hours of tennis every week will account for the loss of 25 pounds in a year. Still, you can't afford to be thoughtless about your diet. If you walk one mile a day, you'll lose 6 pounds of fat in a year, but if you increase your food intake by only 100 calories a day, which is the equivalent of a slice of lightly buttered bread, you will gain more than 10 pounds in a year.

Q. *Can you sweat away fat in a sauna, or by using a sauna belt or rubberized suit?*

A. No. You can temporarily lose weight in a sauna, or by wearing a sauna belt or rubberized suit, but the loss is body water, not fat. Rubberized suits (and saunas) interfere with the body's temperature-regulating system by keeping body heat trapped inside the suit thus causing profuse sweating. However, once you begin to eat and drink, the body reabsorbs the fluid and body weight goes back up. Note that middle-aged and older persons should be careful in a sauna or rubberized suit because of the dangers of heat exhaustion. This is especially true after exercise, when the body is trying to reduce body temperature.

Q. *How do I guide myself when I eat out?*

A. Learn to analyze what you order. Keep your food exchanges in mind. For example, a beef pie, besides a meat exchange, would also include a bread exchange in the crust, and fat and vegetable exchanges in the sauce. Your only extras should be fresh vegetables and fruit.

Q. *Is there an allowance for snack foods?*

A. No. All common snack foods, such as sweet rolls, doughnuts, candy, potato chips, peanuts, etc., are too high in calories and as a result disrupt weight loss. If you need snacks, save a piece of fruit from lunch for midafternoon and a slice of bread from dinner to toast at bedtime. And then remember that most fresh vegetables are free at any time of the day.

Also try a little between-meals exercising. We often reach for food because we are feeling a kind of "false fatigue." Perhaps we've been sitting in one spot so long that we need to get the blood flowing. A brief, vigorous workout should energize you and help you put off your appetite until mealtime.

Q. *What if I can't help myself and go off my diet occasionally?*

A. If you are caught up with a strong craving for something that is not on your diet, enjoy it. But don't let it happen often.

Q. *Can I substitute a cocktail for one of the exchanges?*

A. No, because alcohol contains no nutrients. Also, remember that alcohol is high in calories. For example, an ounce of 80-proof liquor accounts for 80 calories; 100-proof liquor, 100 calories. Mixed drinks usually have more calories per ounce.

Alcohol calories also present a special problem because they are powerful calories. Alcohol calories oxidize quickly, which means that if you are eating and drinking at the same time, food calories must wait and therefore be stored as fat. Your best choice in a social drink is lemonade made with a nonsugar sweetener or a diet soda.

Q. *If I miss a meal, can I make it up later in the day?*

A. Missing a meal occasionally is not critical to your nutritional health. But don't eat "twice as much" at a later meal. Stick with your diet.

Q. *What if I decide to go below 1,200 calories a day?*

A. The advantage in the 1,200-calorie diet is that it's nutritionally sound and establishes good basic eating habits. If you choose to reduce this further, consult your physician. If your physician approves, you will likely be required to take nutrient supplements.

Q. *Does the diet take into consideration restrictions on cholesterol?*

A. If your physician has recommended that you limit cholesterol, you'll have no problem adapting the exchange lists to his instructions. If you are a self-designated cholesterol (and saturated-fat) watcher, then you'll have to follow some guidelines in selecting food because you can't avoid cholesterol unless you are a vegetarian, for even the leanest of meats has some cholesterol. However, with forethought, you can try to limit yourself to about 300 mg. of cholesterol a day, which is the recommendation of the American Heart Association to help prevent heart and vascular disease.

As a general guideline, assume that a three-ounce portion of any one of these—lean beef, lamb, pork, turkey, fish, and chicken—contain about 70 mg. of cholesterol. Fish, except for shellfish, is your best bet because it is especially lean, and what fat it does have is polyunsaturated. Poultry is your next best bet. Finally, remember that no matter how lean the cut of red meat, it still has from 5 to 10 percent saturated fat.

In dairy foods seek out the skimmed and low-fat dairy products to eliminate saturated fat and cholesterol.

When using fats for cooking or to spread on bread, use vegetable oils and spreads made of liquid vegetable oil, especially safflower, corn, cottonseed, and soybean oils.

Of course, you are always home free with vegetables, legumes, fruits, and grains.

THE FOOD-EXCHANGE SYSTEM

On a nutritionally balanced 1,200-calorie diet, you are allowed all of the following in a single day:

3 fruit exchanges

4 bread exchanges

7 meat exchanges

3 fat exchanges

2 milk exchanges

1 vegetable exchange—List B

Vegetable-Exchange List A—
   as desired

Free-Exchange List—as
   desired

Daily Menu Plans

Although you may plan meals to your taste from the above, the recommended pattern for three meals would be:

BREAKFAST

1 fruit exchange
1 bread exchange
1 meat exchange
1 fat exchange
1 milk exchange

LUNCH

3 meat exchanges
2 bread exchanges
Vegetable-Exchange List A—
    as desired
1 fruit exchange
1 fat exchange

SUPPER OR DINNER

3 meat exchanges
1 bread exchange
1 vegetable exchange—List B
Vegetable-Exchange List A—
    as desired
1 fruit exchange
1 fat exchange
1 milk exchange

If you follow the above menu patterns, you will be assured variety and balanced nutrition. You may make exchanges among the three meals as long as it all balances out by the end of the day. For example, if you eat an extra bread exchange in the bun with a hamburger, you should omit a bread exchange from another meal. Or if you take a double portion of potatoes, then you would also omit a slice of bread.

FRUIT-EXCHANGE LIST
Juices and Fruits

None of these fruits and juices should contain added sugar or fat. Each portion as designated contains approximately 10 grams of carbohydrates, negligible protein and fat, and 40 calories. One portion of juice may be substituted for one portion of fruit.

Juices

Juice	Portion Size	Juice	Portion Size
Apple	⅓ cup	Cranberry	1½ cup
Banana-orange	⅓ cup	Grape	¼ cup
Blended	½ cup	Grapefruit	½ cup

Juice	Portion Size	Juice	Portion Size
Mango	⅓ cup	Prune	¼ cup
Orange	½ cup	Tangerine	½ cup
Papaya	⅓ cup	Tomato	1 cup
Pineapple	⅓ cup	Vegetable	1 cup

WARNING: Avoid nectars and sweetened juices.

Fruits

Fruit	Portion Size	Fruit	Portion Size
Apple		Cherries	
Baked	1 small	Bing	½ cup
Canned	½ cup	Royal Anne	½ cup
Dried	1 small	Sour	½ cup
Fresh	1 small		
Sauce		Cranberries, raw	1 cup
Canned	½ cup	Currants	
Cooked	½ cup	Dried	2 tbsp.
		Fresh	½ cup
Apricots			
Canned	4 halves	Dates	2
Cooked	4 halves		
Dried	4 halves	Figs	
Fresh	2 medium	Canned	2 large
		Cooked	2 large
Banana		Dried	1 small
Sliced	½ cup	Fresh	2 large
Whole (with			
skin)	½ small	Fruit cocktail	½ cup
Berries, canned		Fruit cup, fresh	½ cup
Blackberries	⅔ cup		
Blueberries	½ cup	Grapefruit	
Raspberries,		Halves	1 small
red	⅔ cup	Sections	½ cup
Strawberries	⅔ cup		
		Grapes	
		Green seedless	½ cup
Berries, raw		Tokay	½ cup
Blackberries	1 cup		
Blueberries	⅔ cup	Lemon, fresh	1 large
Loganberries	½ cup		
Raspberries,		Mango	½ small
black	1 cup		
Strawberries	1 cup	Melon	
		Cantaloupe	¼ (6-in. diameter)

Fruit	Portion Size	Fruit	Portion Size
Honeydew	⅛ medium	Pineapple	
Watermelon	1 cup	Canned, slices	2 small
		Chunks	½ cup
Nectarine	1 large	Crushed	⅓ cup
		Fresh, chunks	½ cup
Orange			
Sections	½ cup	Plantain	⅓ small
Whole	1 small		
		Plums	
Papaya	⅓ medium	Green gage	2 medium
		Purple	2 medium
Peach			
Canned	2 halves	Prunes	
Dried	2 halves	Canned	2 medium
Fresh		Cooked	2 medium
Sliced	½ cup	Dried	2 medium
Whole	1 medium		
		Raisins	2 tbsp.
Pear			
Canned	2 halves	Rhubarb	
Dried	2 halves	Canned	1 cup
Fresh		Fresh	any amount
Sliced	½ cup		
Whole	1 small	Tangerine	
		Sections	½ cup
		Whole	1 large

Special suggestions:

1. Lemon or lime juices or slices may be used as flavoring or garnish.

2. Parsley or mint may be used as a garnish.

3. Any spice or herb that does not contain added sugar may be used.

4. Sugar substitute may be used as desired.

5. Calorie-restricted fruit or calorie-restricted juice in the tables may be combined with plain unsweetened gelatin to be used as a dessert.

6. If fruit is used as a salad, plain unsweetened gelatin may be used as a dessert.

BREAD-EXCHANGE LIST

Cereal, Bread, and Starchy Foods

Each portion as designated for the cereal, bread, buns, crackers, potatoes, and potato substitutes contains approximately 15 grams of carbohydrates, 2 grams of protein, negligible fat, and 68 calories.

Cereal

Cooked—½ cup	Ready to serve—¾ cup
Barley, pearled	Bran
Corn meal	Bran flakes
"Cream of Rice"	"Cheerios"
"Cream of Wheat"	Cornflakes
Farina	"Grape Nuts Flakes"
Hominy grits	"Kix"
"Maltex"	"Muffets"
"Malt-O-Meal"	"Post Toasties"
"Maypo"	Rice, flaked
Millet	"Rice Krispies"
Oatmeal	Rice, puffed
"Pabena"	Wheat, flaked
"Pablum"	Wheat, puffed
"Pettijohns"	Wheat, shredded
"Ralston"	Wheat corn, malt flavor
Rice	"Wheaties"
Tapioca	
"Wheatena"	
Wheat meal	

WARNING: Avoid sugar- and chocolate-coated cereals.

NOTE: You may also include any variety of enriched cereal prepared without added fat or sugar. You may add salt or sugar substitute to cereals. However, fruits, milk, butter, or margarine used with cereal must be deducted from the total amounts allowed on the Daily Menu Plans.

Bread, Crackers, Rolls

Item	Portion Size	Item	Portion Size
Biscuits	1 (2-in. diameter)	Wheat	
		Cracked	1 slice
		Whole	1 slice
Bread or toast		White	1 slice
Dilly	1 thin slice		
French or Vienna	1 thin slice	Bread crumbs, dry	¼ cup
Italian	1 thin slice		
Pumpernickel	1 thin slice	Buns	
Rye	1 thin slice	Frankfurter	½
		Hamburger	½

Item	Portion Size	Item	Portion Size
Cornbread	1 (1½-in. cube)	Soda	3 (2½-in. square)
Crackers		"Triscuit"	3
Bran wafer	2	"Uneeda" biscuit	3
Crouton	½ cup	"Vegetable Thin"	13
Graham	2 (2½-in. square)	"Venus" wafer	3
Matzoh	1 (6-in. diameter)	"Waverly" wafer	6
Oyster	½ cup(20)	Flour	2½ tbsp.
"Ritz"	7	Muffin	1 (2-in. diameter)
Cheese	7		
Regular	7	Roll, dinner or hard	1
"Round Thin"	6 (1½-in. diameter)		
Saltine	5 (2-in. square)	Tortilla, yellow or white corn	3 (6-in. diameter)

WARNING: Avoid Boston, cinnamon, and raisin breads; coffee cakes; fried cornbread; doughnuts; hushpuppies; icing; Danish pastries; sweet rolls; or sugar on or in bread or rolls.

Potatoes and Potato Substitutes

Item	Portion Size	Item	Portion Size
Beans		Hominy	
Baked	¼ cup	Grits	½ cup
Dried	½ cup	Whole	½ cup
Kidney	½ cup	Macaroni	½ cup
Lima		Noodles	½ cup
Baby, immature	½ cup	Parsnips	⅔ cup
Mature	½ cup	Peas	
Navy	½ cup	Black-eyed, dried	½ cup
Pinto	½ cup	Dried, split	½ cup
Red	½ cup	Field	½ cup
Chickpeas	½ cup	Potato	
Corn		Sweet	¼ cup
On the cob	1 small ear	White	
Popped	1 cup	Mashed	½ cup
Sweet, white or yellow	⅓ cup	Whole	1 (2-in. diameter)

Item	Portion Size	Item	Portion Size
Yam	¼ cup	White	½ cup
Rice		Wild	½ cup
Brown	½ cup	Spaghetti	½ cup

Special suggestions:

1. Potato or a substitute may be prepared with salt, pepper, vinegar, lemon or lime juice, any spices or herbs, clear broth, bouillon, tomato juice, sugar substitutes, or seasoning not containing fat or sugar.

2. Milk, butter, or substitute used with potato or potato substitute must be deducted from the total amounts allowed on the Daily Menu Plans. Polyunsaturated fats may be used with potato or potato substitute on fat-controlled diets.

FAT-EXCHANGE LIST

Fat, Butter, Margarine, Oil, and Other Fatty Foods

Each portion as designated below contains approximately 5 grams of fat, and 45 calories.

Item	Portion Size	Item	Portion Size
Avocado	⅛ (4-in. diameter)	Oils	
		Coconut	1 tsp.
Butter or		Corn	1 tsp.
margarine	1 tsp.	Cottonseed	1 tsp.
Bacon, crisp	1 slice	Olive	1 tsp.
Bacon fat	1 tsp.	Peanut	1 tsp.
Cream		Safflower	1 tsp.
Light, 12%	3 tbsp.	Sesame seed	1 tsp.
Heavy, 30%	4 tsp.	Soybean	1 tsp.
Cream cheese	1 tbsp.	Sunflower seed	1 tsp.
French dressing	1 tbsp.	Vegetable	1 tsp.
Lard	1 tsp.	Olives	5 small
Mayonnaise	1 tsp.	Pork, salt (no lean)	½-in. cube
Nuts	6 small		

NOTE: If you use margarines high in polyunsaturated fats instead of butter, please remember that the number of calories is the equivalent of butter.

MEAT-EXCHANGE LIST

Meat, Fish, Poultry, Cheese, Egg, and Other Protein

Each of the meat exchanges, or the meat-protein equivalent, contains approximately 7 grams of protein, 5 grams of fat, and 73 calories.

Item	Portion Size	Item	Portion Size
Beef		Herring	1 oz.
Corned	1 oz.	Lobster	1 oz. (¼ cup)
Dried	1 oz.		
Frankfurter	1	Mackerel	1 oz.
Ground	1 oz.	Oysters	5 small
Roast, any cut	1 oz.	Perch	1 oz.
Short ribs	1 oz.	Pompano	1 oz.
Steak, any cut	1 oz.	Salmon	¼ cup
Stew cuts	1 oz.	Sardines	3 medium
Veal		Scallops	5 small
Chops	1 oz.	Shad	1 oz.
Cutlets	1 oz.	Shrimp	5 small
Ground	1 oz.	Swordfish	1 oz.
Roast	1 oz.	Trout	1 oz.
Stew cuts	1 oz.	Tuna	¼ cup
Cheese		Whitefish	1 oz.
American	1 oz.	Frog legs	1 oz.
Bleu	1 oz.	Lamb	
Cheddar	1 oz.	Chops	1 oz.
Cottage, dry	¼ cup	Roast	1 oz.
Roquefort	1 oz.	Stew cuts	1 oz.
Swiss	1 oz.	Peanut butter*	2 tbsp.
Egg	1	Pork	
Fish and shellfish		Canadian bacon	1 oz.
Bass	1 oz.	Chops	1 oz.
Bluefish	1 oz.	Frankfurter	1
Catfish	1 oz.	Ham	
Clams	5 small	Ground	1 oz.
Cod	1 oz.	Roast	1 oz.
Crab	¼ cup	Steak	1 oz.
Flounder	1 oz.	Roast	1 oz.
Haddock	1 oz.	Poultry and game	
Halibut	1 oz.	Chicken	1 oz.

* Peanut butter should be limited to one exchange daily. If more than one exchange of peanut butter is used, 5 grams of carbohydrate should be deducted per exchange used in excess.

Item	Portion Size	Item	Portion Size
Cornish hen	1 oz.	Venison	1 oz.
Duck	1 oz.	Variety meat	
Goose	1 oz.	Brain	1 oz.
Guinea	1 oz.	Cold cut	1 slice
Pheasant	1 oz.	Heart	1 oz.
Quail	1 oz.	Kidney	1 oz.
Rabbit	1 oz.	Liver	1 oz.
Squab	1 oz.	Sweetbreads	1 oz.
Squirrel	1 oz.	Tongue	1 oz.
Turkey	1 oz.		

WARNING: Avoid meats prepared with fat or sugar, beef and pork sausages, spareribs, pork that has not been trimmed or drained, bacon, cream cheese, meats or meat substitutes fried in fat, mixed meat dishes unless recipe has been evaluated for fat content, and gravies and sauces made with fat, cream, or sugar.

Special Suggestions:

1. Meat should be trimmed of excess fat and cooked by broiling, boiling, baking, roasting, or simmering in frying pan lightly brushed with shortening to prevent sticking.

2. Meat may be prepared with salt, pepper, vinegar, lemon or lime juice or slices, any spices or herbs, clear broth, bouillon, tomato juice, seasoning not containing fat or sugar, tomato sauce, or gravy (no fat, flour, or eggs).

3. Three ounces, or 90 grams, of cooked meat or meat substitute is considered a serving. However, other weights or portions may be indicated on the specific Daily Menu Plan.

4. Three ounces of cooked meat is equivalent to 4 ounces of raw meat. Allow 40- to 50-percent increase for bones and skin when using poultry.

VEGETABLE-EXCHANGE LISTS

When prepared without fat or sugar, 1 cup of Group A vegetables contains negligible carbohydrate, protein, and calories, and so these vegetables may be eaten in desired quantities; ½ cup of Group B vegetables contains approximately 7 grams of carbohydrate, 2 grams of protein, and 36 calories, and therefore these vegetables must be measured.

Group A—as desired

Artichokes
Asparagus
Bamboo shoots
Beans
  Green
  Wax
Bean sprouts
Brocolli
Brussels sprouts
Cabbage
Cauliflower
Celery
Chicory
Chives
Cucumbers
Eggplant
Endive
Escarole
Garlic
Greens
Kohlrabi
Lettuce
Mushrooms
Okra
Parsley
Peppers
Pimentos
Radishes
Romaine
Sauerkraut
Spinach
Squash, summer
Tomatoes
Watercress

Group B—½ cup

Beets
Carrots
Onions
Peas, green
Pumpkin
Rutabaga
Squash, winter
Turnip roots
Vegetables, mixed

Special suggestions:

1. Vegetables may be prepared with salt, pepper, vinegar, lemon or lime juice or slices, any spices or herbs and seasoning not containing fat or sugar (although sugar substitute may be used).

2. Milk, butter, or butter substitute used with vegetables must be deducted from the total amounts allowed on the Daily Menu Plans.

3. Fruit served in a salad must also be deducted from the total fruit exchanges allowed.

4. Potato, macaroni, or other substitutes served in a salad must be deducted from the total bread exchanges.

5. Fat in dressings or mayonnaise must also be deducted from the day's total fat allowance.

Special Salad-Dressing Recipes

You can prepare your own salad dressings with herbs or spices that don't contain sugar. Oil and vinegar, or mayonnaise, may be used by deducting one fat exchange for each teaspoon of oil or mayonnaise used.

Following are six salad dressings of which one portion— 1 tablespoon—contains negligible calories (or about 15 calories per tablespoon):

French Dressing

1 tsp.	Dry mustard
1½ tsp.	Salt
1 tsp.	Onion juice
1 tbsp.	Paprika
1 cup	Vinegar
¼ cup	Water
2	Raw eggs
	Sugar substitute to taste

Combine dry ingredients and onion juice. Add vinegar and water and beat. Add eggs and beat thoroughly. Add sugar substitute.

Fruit French Dressing

Add to 1 cup of French Dressing:

2 tbsp.	Pineapple juice
2 tbsp.	Grapefruit juice
1 tsp.	Lemon juice
	Sugar substitute to taste

Fruit Salad Dressing

2 tbsp.	Cornstarch
2½ tbsp.	Water
2	Eggs
½ cup	Pineapple juice
½ cup	Orange juice
2 tbsp.	Lemon juice
	Sugar substitute to taste

Mix cornstarch and water to make a paste. Add eggs; mix thoroughly. Combine juices and heat to boiling in top of double boiler. Gradually add starch-egg mixture, stirring constantly. Cook until thick and add sugar substitute to taste.

Transparent Dressing

1 tsp.	Dry mustard
2 tbsp.	Cornstarch
¼ tsp.	Salt
½ cup	Vinegar
2 tbsp.	Minced onion
1⅓ cups	Water
	Sugar substitute to taste

Mix all ingredients except sugar substitute in a saucepan. Stir until mixture boils and keep stirring for 2 minutes. Add sugar substitute to taste.

Vinegar Dressing

1 cup	Vinegar
½ tsp.	Salt
½ tsp.	Dry mustard
½ tsp.	Paprika

Combine ingredients in a jar and shake well.

Zero Dressing

1 cup	Tomato juice
4 tbsp.	Lemon juice or vinegar
2 tbsp.	Minced onion
¼ tsp.	Salt
	Pepper to taste
	Sugar substitute to taste

Combine ingredients in a jar and shake well.

MILK-EXCHANGE LIST

Item	Portion Size	Item	Portion Size
Buttermilk, skim	1 cup	2%-fat milk* ("low-fat")	1 cup
Dried/powder skim milk	¼ cup	Whole milk**	1 cup
Evaporated milk**	½ cup	Yogurt, plain**	1 cup
Skim milk	1 cup		

NOTE: Milk when used in the preparation of foods must be deducted from the amount of milk allowed in the Daily Menu Plans.

* Omit one fat exchange from diet.
** Omit two fat exchanges from diet.

FREE-EXCHANGE LIST (NEGLIGIBLE CALORIES)

Bouillon
Broth, fat-free
Coffee
Cranberries with noncaloric
  sweetener
Gelatin, low calorie
Lemon

Lemonade with noncaloric
  sweetener
Mustard
Pickles, dill/sour
Tea
Rhubarb with noncaloric
  sweetener
Vinegar

CHAPTER 6

Testing and Recording Your Progress

There are a number of ways to measure your fitness progress. Some are subjective—feeling better, sleeping better, and enjoying a new and higher level of energy. And some are mundane: If you're slimming down, you may suddenly discover that your trousers or skirts are getting baggy. All of this is to the good, but not good enough to measure your progress and protect your health.

TESTING FOR WEIGHT CONTROL

Weighing In Regularly

The few seconds that it takes to step on a bathroom scale and record your weight is very important. It's a simple act that can save you a lot of grief. For example, if you're dieting, a loss of up to about two pounds a week is considered safe. If you're dropping weight a lot faster, you should check with your physician.

On the other hand, if you have been relaxing a little in your dieting, the scale may alert you before you have gained more than a couple of pounds. If you are not weighing in regularly, you may have to reckon with the sudden discovery that you have gained six to ten pounds of undesirable fat.

Begin by drawing up a simple chart and record your weight once a week. Monday morning is strongly recommended as the time to weigh in at the Academy because it reminds cadets to control their appetites over the weekend. Weighing yourself at the same time of day will assure a more accurate indication of your weight loss.

Always weigh in on the same bathroom scale. While the

average bathroom scale is not as accurate as the more expensive scales found in a physician's office, they are satisfactory indicators of weight loss or gain.

Body Measurements for Men and Women

While the scale will record your weight loss and then help you maintain a desirable weight, body tape measurements are your best indicators of figure control.

Your tape measurements will indicate reductions in your waistline, hips, etc. You'll also find that a reduction in tape measurements corresponds to the reduction in body weight as measured on your bathroom scale.

When possible, measurements should be taken by another person. Failing this, measure yourself in front of a full-length mirror. Maintain a balanced posture. Use either a vinyl or a plastic-coated tape measure. Take measurements at the beginning of the program and then at six-week intervals, always using the original tape. Directions below are the same for men and women, except for the pectoralis measurement, which is for women only. (Refer to diagram on next page.)

Record the circumference of your:

1. *Chest:*
    a. Pectoralis—directly under arms and above bust (women only)
    b. Largest part of bust or chest
2. *Upper arm*—midway between elbow and shoulder joint:
    a. Relaxed
    b. Contracted
3. *Midriff*—largest part between bust and waist
4. *Waist*—smallest part
5. *Abdomen*—largest part or two inches below navel
6. *Hips*—largest part of buttocks
7. *Upper thigh*—directly under buttocks
8. *Lower thigh*—with feet together, four inches above top edge of knee
9. *Calf*—largest part

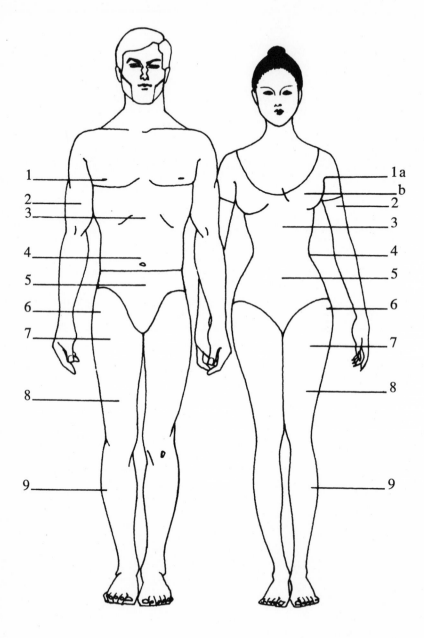

Recommended Girth Proportions for Men and Women

What should be the size of your chest in proportion to your hips—or the size of your calves in proportion to your ankles? Exercise and weight control will help balance the proportions of your body, but it is your genes that dictate the "normal" size of different parts of an individual's body. If you are concerned about your body proportions, or question whether you have lost enough fat, use the following guide to girth proportions, which are based on measurements of a large number of men and women who are considered well proportioned.

Chest or bust: Circumference of chest at nipple line and at midpoint of normal breath

Men: Same as hip circumference

Women: Same as hip circumference

Waist: Minimal abdominal girth, below rib cage and just above top of hip bone

Men: Five to seven inches less than chest or hips

Women: Ten inches less than bust or hips

Hips: Level of pubic bone on front and including largest part of buttocks

Men: Same as chest

Women: Same as bust

Thighs: Upper part of thighs, directly under buttocks and just below fold

Men: Eight to ten inches less than waist

Women: Six to seven inches less than waist

Calves: Circumference of largest part of calves

Men: Seven to eight inches less than thighs

Women: Six to seven inches less than thighs

Ankles: Minimal circumference usually just above ankle bone

Men: Six to seven inches less than calves

Women: Five to six inches less than calves

Upper Arm: Circumference midway between elbow and shoulder joint, with arm extended and palm up

Men: Twice the circumference of wrist when wrist is measured at minimal circumference, just above wrist bone

Women: Same as for men

TESTING FOR CARDIORESPIRATORY IMPROVEMENT

As you would expect, the best and most sophisticated testing of CR (cardiorespiratory) efficiency requires equipment that is used in the laboratory of an exercise physiologist. However, there is a reasonably good test that can be applied in the home, based on two factors that were noted in Chapter 3, The Walk/Run Plan.

Generally a heart that beats more slowly at rest and work is more efficient. The slower rhythm gives the heart more time to fill with blood and thereby pump more blood (oxygen and nutrients) per beat through the body. Another test of increased CR efficiency is a quicker rate of recovery after you have exerted yourself. For example, if you have to run hard in a game or sprint for a train, the less time it takes for your heartbeat to return to normal the better your CR health. Both of these tests can be performed in the home under "controlled conditions." The only expertise you need is being able to take your own pulse which you learned in Chapter 3, The Walk/Run Plan.

The Step Test

Equipment required:
- A watch with a sweep hand to take your pulse
- A sturdy bench or chair, 16 or 17 inches high, that will not tip when you stand on it (instead of a chair or bench, you may use the second step in a staircase if it is 16 or 17 inches from the floor)
- A chart similar to the one shown here

RESTING HEART RATE AND HEART-RATE RECOVERY CHART

Pretraining
Date: ———

1. Resting
       H.R. ——— × 6 = ———
       (10 sec.)
2. Immediately after exercise
       H.R. ——— × 6 = ———
       (10 sec.)
3. After 2 min.
       H.R. ——— × 6 = ———
       (10 sec.)
4. After 3 min.
       H.R. ——— × 6 = ———
       (10 sec.)
5. After 4 min.
       H.R. ——— × 6 = ———
       (10 sec.)

After Fourth Week
Date: ———

1. Resting
       H.R. ——— × 6 = ———
       (10 sec.)
2. Immediately after exercise
       H.R. ——— × 6 = ———
       (10 sec.)
3. After 2 min.
       H.R. ——— × 6 = ———
       (10 sec.)
4. After 3 min.
       H.R. ——— × 6 = ———
       (10 sec.)
5. After 4 min.
       H.R. ——— × 6 = ———
       (10 sec.)

After Eighth Week
Date: ———

1. Resting
       H.R. ——— × 6 = ———
       (10 sec.)
2. Immediately after exercise
       H.R. ——— × 6 = ———
       (10 sec.)
3. After 2 min.
       H.R. ——— × 6 = ———
       (10 sec.)
4. After 3 min.
       H.R. ——— × 6 = ———
       (10 sec.)
5. After 4 min.
       H.R. ——— × 6 = ———
       (10 sec.)

After Twelfth Week
Date: ———

1. Resting
       H.R. ——— × 6 = ———
       (10 sec.)
2. Immediately after exercise
       H.R. ——— × 6 = ———
       (10 sec.)
3. After 2 min.
       H.R. ——— × 6 = ———
       (10 sec.)
4. After 3 min.
       H.R. ——— × 6 = ———
       (10 sec.)
5. After 4 min.
       H.R. ——— × 6 = ———
       (10 sec.)

You should test your CR efficiency at four-week intervals. Preferably record the first test before you begin the Walk/Run Plan.

1. Take your heart rate at rest which was explained in Chapter 3. To be certain that your H.R. (heart rate) at rest is consistent throughout the tests, you must see that the conditions are the same. Your H.R. is affected by many things during the day. It starts off at the lowest rate in the morning after awakening and before you get out of bed, then it goes up and down during the day depending on what you are doing. When you eat, smoke, or drink, your H.R. goes up. If you are cold or hot, get excited or angry, it will rise. Therefore, in order to record a valid resting H.R. for comparative purposes, you should sit down and take your resting H.R. at the same time of the day, and at least two hours after eating, drinking, or smoking, as well as in an environment free of excitement or anger. Take your H.R. for ten seconds and record in line 1 of the chart.

2. The Step Test itself is performed in a four-count movement:
   (1) Step up onto chair (or stairway) with left foot
   (2) Bring your right foot up next to your left foot
   (3) Step down and back to floor with left foot
   (4) Bring right foot down to floor next to left foot

Repeat this exercise 30 times per minute for two minutes. When finished, immediately sit down on the chair or staircase, and take your H.R. for ten seconds and enter in line 2 of chart.

3. Continue sitting rest until a total of two minutes has elapsed from the moment you stopped exercising. Again take your pulse for ten seconds and enter figure in line 3.

4. Continue sitting rest until a total of three minutes has elapsed from the time you stopped exercising. Take your H.R. for ten seconds and enter in line 4.

5. After a total of four minutes of sitting rest, take your H.R. again for ten seconds and enter in line 5.

Now that the test is completed, multiply each figure by six to get your heart rate for one minute at each step of the test.

Interpreting the Test

The first test, in the pretraining period, means little by itself. However, when you repeat the test at four-week intervals, after you are training with the Walk/Run program, you should have three different kinds of evidence of your progress:

First, your resting H.R. (line 1) will get lower.

Second, your H.R. during exercise (line 2) will not go as high, which indicates that your heart isn't working as hard to perform the same amount of work.

Third, your H.R. will recover to your resting H.R. sooner (lines 3, 4, and 5). By the end of 12 weeks your pulse should return to the resting H.R. within two or three minutes after you have stopped the exercise.

As you continue to walk/run through the intermediate and maintenance levels of exercises, your resting H.R. will begin leveling off. This means that you are approaching your peak fitness. Remember that conditioning cannot be stored but begins to disappear within 72 hours after you stop training. You must train habitually at least three times a week to build fitness and two times a week to maintain fitness.

SECTION II

Personal Conditioning Program for Other Ages

CHAPTER 7

The Early Years
–up to Age 12

Friends of your son drop by and ask him to come out and play ball. Your son makes an excuse, explaining he has something else to do. Perhaps he would prefer to play ball with his friends, but he's embarrassed because he's a little clumsy at catching and throwing.

Your daughter, who has never been athletically inclined, decides she will take tennis lessons. For a while she appears to be getting along fairly well, but then she quits. As it turns out, she's hitting the ball fairly well, but when it comes to moving around the court, she feels so awkward that she's become self-conscious. Like many other girls, she's never learned how to run.

There are tens of thousands of youngsters like these. We see some of them at West Point. They are normal and eager to participate in sports, but they have to work twice as hard as anyone else to complete the same motion, because they have not learned in their early years the basics of good coordination, balance, and agility.

The four years of physical education at the Academy are intense, and while we can increase a cadet's strength, endurance, and cardiorespiratory fitness, there's little we can do about their motor coordination. It's just too late. There are some physical functions that need learning and practice in the early years of childhood. It's often then or never.

Are Parents at Fault?

It's always presumptuous to tell parents that they are neglecting their children, and so this starts off with an apology. However, one study after another finds that a majority of our young men are physically unfit, and the fitness rating of young women is just about at the disaster level. A lot of this is a result of general ignorance and sociocultural bias.

Let's look at some of the reasons parents offer when explaining their neglect:

"A child learns to play ball when he's ready."

A false notion. Try to teach a 12-year-old boy or girl how to throw a ball correctly. You're not likely to succeed.

"Everyone in my family is clumsy."

Maybe, but each generation has a new set of genes.

"Physical skills come naturally and there's nothing to learn."

Human beings have inherent patterns of movement, but all need practice and improvement.

"The kids will get all the coaching they need in school."

School may be too late. Some physical skills require development in preschool years. And, unfortunately, when a youngster starts school, there's often little help, for few elementary schools have either a budget or staff to be concerned with the physical fitness of children.

"I can understand being concerned about a boy's physical development, but does a girl need it?"

A typical American scene finds parents and daughter watching the son at play—racing, catching, hitting a ball. The family exults in the boy's fitness and skill, but no one thinks about the daughter, either about her fitness or the development of her athletic skills.

What we now know is that our young girls have been neglected by parents and educators. It has been as deliberate and as inexcusable as the Oriental practice of binding a young girl's feet. Both are crippling. It's time to do something about it and we hope that our program will help.

Catching Them Early

We are born with legs, but everyone must go through a crawling, stumbling, and toddling process while learning to walk. We know that even sight is a learning process; if a child is kept in total darkness throughout infancy, he will never learn to see. Similarly, running, jumping, throwing, and striking, although inherent physical patterns, must have an opportunity to develop.

If the patterns are not practiced at the time that they surface naturally, the younger's coordination may be permanently affected.

During the rapid growth in the first two years of life we see simple movement patterns—picking up the head, rising up on hands and knees, crawling, and then toddling. You see the inherent pattern for throwing when the infant throws a milk bottle or rattle out of the crib.

Up to the age of 3 a child will likely throw an object with either the left or right hand. When he begins to favor one hand over the other, the parent should give the youngster a small, soft ball (baseball size) and encourage the child to throw the ball properly. The correct way is to step forward with the foot opposite the throwing hand. For example, when throwing with the right hand, the child should step toward the target with the left foot. Just as you see a baseball pitcher do on television.

By the age of 5, children have reasonably good control of large muscle activities used in locomotion skills such as running, jumping, and climbing. Their hearts are growing rapidly. Girls will be about as big as boys but more mature physically. At this age children need vigorous physical activities, but of short duration because they tire easily.

Parents can help children best in the 3-to-6-year-old range by playing games and encouraging physical activities that are challenging but not frustrating. Examples of such activities are:

1. Teach the child progressively how to jump and then how to run and jump. Begin with a double-legged takeoff and landing without a run. When the jump by itself is mastered, have the child run and jump over a pillow. The third stage is run, jump, and run, so the child learns to run after the jump is completed.

2. Give the child a large, bouncy ball about the size of a basketball. Begin with games that require the child to roll the ball at a target or between the legs of a chair. Teach the child to catch the ball on a bounce from you. Then have the child bounce the ball back to you. When the youngster gets good at bouncing and catching the ball with two hands, start a new game. Let the child learn to dribble the ball with both hands, bouncing it one or three times, and then catching the ball. Gradually, the child will be able to dribble with one hand, although this may not occur before the age of 6.

3. Begin to practice throwing skills with a small ball. You

be the target and catch it with two hands, and then let the child learn to catch with two hands. You will have to throw the ball underhand and carefully. If the ball is too small, try a slightly larger one. Or use a bean bag. Try other shapes of balls, including lightweight footballs. During this practice children are learning to develop hand-eye coordination, and *patience* is the word for the parent.

4. By the age of 3, or preferably before, a child should be introduced to the swimming pool because it will likely make the learning of swimming much easier. Elementary swimming can be taught beginning at the age of 2, and sometimes earlier. At West Point 6 to 10 percent of our entering classes are classified as nonswimmers. We've learned that many of their parents, especially their mothers, are nonswimmers who taught their children to be afraid of water. As a parent you should teach children as young as 12 months old that it can be fun to play in water. Teach a child to respect water but not to fear it.

5. A jungle gym is strongly recommended for the backyard. Children enjoy climbing and swinging from bars, and this is the beginning of the development of upper-body strength.

6. By the age of 6, children like to play games of kickball. Their foot-eye coordination isn't fully developed, but this is a good age to begin practicing body balance along with foot-eye coordination. The ball for this age group should be a light rubber ball rather than a regulation soccer ball. Have them practice kicking with both feet.

7. Age 6 is also a good time to give your child, boy or girl, a hollow plastic bat. Begin practicing by pitching a small plastic ball to the child from a distance of about six feet, using an underhand throw. As the child begins to hit the ball regularly, you can begin moving farther away as you pitch.

8. Remember these key words when working with preschool children:

Patience, because you must not expect quick results.

Persistence, because it will take time and repetition.

Variety, because youngsters will expect you to be imaginative and create a variety of games.

Fun, because the child must enjoy what you are doing together.

Balance

*Ball Dribbling
Hand-Eye Coordination*

Running

Tumbling Stunts

*Pull-Up—Upper Body
or Arm and Shoulder
Girdle Strength*

The 6-Year-Old and School

Most elementary schools cannot be relied on to take on the full responsibility of your child's physical development. Most schools lack facilities, an adequate physical education staff, and the money to get either, but you may be lucky, and it's worth checking into. Ask for a conference with the physical education teacher or ask for straight talk at a PTA meeting.

If you discover that the responsibility is still yours, the stress won't be any worse because a 6-year-old is much like the 5-year-old in terms of physical development. Hand-eye coordination is still difficult because of the slow development of the smaller muscles. Generally, except for the heart and brain, growth is usually slow in the sixth year.

Remember that at the age of 6, girls are not only the equal of boys but may often be more mature emotionally, socially, and physically. Like boys, girls are ready and eager to learn the skills of baseball, softball, basketball, soccer, and gymnastics. This makes the first grade of school a critical year for the 6-year-old girl.

For the first time large numbers of other 6-year-olds are available to the girl for companionship and games. The teacher may send the boys off to play with the boys, while the girls are encouraged to play with girls. There will be boy games and girl games, and then the old sociocultural sex bias may take over. The physically active girl finds herself being asked to slow down, conform, not be a tomboy. And this shouldn't happen.

The 6-year-old girl should be encouraged to learn and play all the games that boys play—not because she will necessarily be playing on the boys' team (although she is likely to play as well if not better than boys do), but so that she at least may fully develop all of her motor skills.

The 7-Year-Old

In the seventh year a child begins to show a higher level of maturity both physically and mentally. Most growth appears to be in the length of arms and legs. Hand-eye and foot-eye coordination show marked improvement. The 7-year-old shows more daring on the jungle gym, and this should be encouraged in girls as well as boys. Girls, like boys, must continue to develop the upper-torso strength that is necessary to handle their body weight.

In the seventh year test your child's flexibility in the hamstring muscles (back side of the thighs) and the lower back. Have your child sit on the floor, feet against a wall. Then ask him to bend forward, touch the wall, and hold for three seconds. During the test you must help him keep his knees flat against the floor. If he cannot pass the flexibility test, begin the exercises that are discussed in Chapter 4, Flexibility.

Look for problems that lead to poor posture in the seventh year. Chapter 11, Posture, will direct you to the most common problems, but be especially alert for a big curve in the lower-back area, which is a sign of forward pelvic tilt. Also check the carriage of the head to make certain it isn't being carried far forward in the "hangdog" position. Try to make posture correction a game. Don't nag. Never correct a child's posture when you're angry.

If you wish, during the seventh year you can begin encouraging your child to practice some of the items on the physical-fitness test of the American Alliance of Health, Physical Education and Recreation, which appears at the end of this chapter.

GOALS FOR THE 7-YEAR-OLD

Flexed-Arm Hang	Bent-Leg Situps	Standing Long Jump	50-Yard Dash	600-Yard Run/Walk
Hold 25 sec. to 35 sec.	25 to 35 in 60 sec.	3'10" to 4'6"	9 sec. to 8.5 sec.	2 min. 30 sec. to 2 min. 15 sec.

NOTE: See detailed directions for these test exercises at end of chapter.

If your 7-year-old can't perform at this level, it may be a signal that a little more encouragement is needed, but you must remember also that different children develop at different rates. With patience and persistence and by making it fun, your child should be able to improve.

The 8-Year-Old

Growth continues to be slow during the eighth year, but there is a surge of improvement and confidence in hand-eye and foot-eye coordination. Children become more daring and accidents may occur, but parents should try to keep from being overprotective.

By the time a child is 8 years old, he's ready to use a bat and a racquet. All competitive sports become exciting. Also, this is a good age to start gymnastics under professional supervision because older children find some tumbling events frightening and difficult to master.

GOALS FOR THE 8-YEAR-OLD

Flexed-Arm Hang	Bent-Leg Situps	Standing Long Jump	50-Yard Dash	600-Yard Run/Walk
Hold 30 sec. to 40 sec.	28 to 38 in 60 sec.	4'0" to 4'10"	8.9 sec. to 8.4 sec.	2 min. 25 sec. to 2 min. 10 sec.

NOTE: See detailed directions for these test exercises at end of chapter.

The 9-Year-Old

Growth and coordination continue to improve in the ninth year, but what really distinguishes the 9-year-old from younger children is the development of athletic poise and the desire to improve athletic skills. Team sports and competition become very important, but this is not the time to begin specializing in one sport. Let's look objectively at some of the group activities of particular appeal to this age group:

1. *Swimming* for most adults is a noncompetitive activity that one enjoys at his own pace. However, as a group competitive sport swimming is an altogether different activity and very demanding. The coach will likely ask for most of the child's free time all through the year, and you will likely find that the starting age for competitive swimming is down to age 6. For the few children who may grow up to make the Olympic team all of the work involved may be worthwhile, but for millions of others the demand on a child's time may be excessive.

Of course, most sports require dedication and specialization to reach the Olympic level, but no sport should require that a child be committed at so early an age.

2. *Baseball* as youngsters know it in the Little League program is valuable when kept in proper perspective. It's developmental when all members of the team, not just the most skillful, play a part of every game. Also, parents should recognize that baseball at its best is neither a vigorous sport nor one that comes

close to comprehensive conditioning. In reality, players do a lot of standing while waiting for someone else to make a play.

3. *Gymnastics* is an excellent activity to develop agility, flexibility, and strength, especially in the upper torso. The problem here is chiefly a matter of budget, being able to afford the expert coaching that is necessary to have a safe, developmental program.

Gymnastics should not be a child's only sport activity because its value is limited once school years are over. However, some gymnastic skills are an asset in learning lifetime sports. Also, running, which should be part of every gymnastics course, is valuable in developing the cardiorespiratory system.

4. *Football* is a risk for children up to the age of 12 and 14 because bones and joints are not yet ready to take the pounding. On the other hand, the 9-year-old may well be ready to practice passing, catching, running, punting, and kicking, and to play touch football.

5. *Soccer* is an excellent developmental activity for the legs, the cardiorespiratory system, balance, and foot-eye coordination. Many of soccer's skills can be transferred to other sports, including football, baseball, tennis, handball, and squash. Soccer is highly recommended and, of course, preferable to football as a developmental sport for children under 14, although it makes little contribution to the development of the upper body.

6. *Basketball,* like soccer, is also a good all-around developmental sport. Be cautioned that basketball can become obsessive and take excessive time because the primary skills such as shooting and dribbling require long hours of practice. Despite all the work, basketball is another sport that fails to develop upper-body strength.

We continue to refer to upper body strength because over the years our experience and studies at West Point have convinced us that most American youngsters, particularly women, are underdeveloped through the shoulder, chest, and back muscles. The ninth year is a good time to get both boys and girls started on pull-ups and push-ups to build upper-body strength and endurance.

To help children get started with pull-ups, you can begin by teaching them what we call "negative pull-ups" at West Point. This exercise begins with the chin over the bar; then the child slowly lowers his body to the straight-arm hang. You can lift the child up to the bar each time, or he can use a box or stool to climb up.

Straight Arm Hang

Completed Pull-Up

If a child can't immediately do push-ups from the floor, he can start at an easier level by pushing off a sturdy table or desk. Let him build up his strength until he can do 35 to 40 push-ups off a table, and then he can move to a lower object, such as a chair, then to a stool, and finally to the floor.

GOALS FOR THE 9-YEAR-OLD

Flexed-Arm Hang	Bent-Leg Situps	Standing Long Jump	50-Yard Dash	600-Yard Run/Walk
Hold 35 sec. to 50 sec.	30 to 40 in 60 sec.	4'2" to 5'	8.7 sec. to 8.2 sec.	2 min. 20 sec. to 2 min. 5 sec.

NOTE: See detailed directions for these test exercises at end of chapter.

The 10- and the 11-Year-Old

In the preadolescent period girls are still more mature physically than boys but will shortly lose this edge. At puberty boys go into a growth spurt and average out taller than girls. In addition, the male hormone, testosterone, spurs rapid development of the boy's bulky muscles, while the female hormone, estrogen, inhibits the development of muscle tissue in young women.

The young girl becoming a woman has the most at stake. If she believes the sociocultural sex bias that says vigor and physical activity are defeminizing, she will then be doubly handicapped. On the other hand, if she chooses the equality route, she can maintain the same physical conditioning program as young men.

GOALS FOR THE 10- AND THE 11-YEAR-OLD

	Flexed Arm Hang or Pull-ups	Bent-Leg Situps	Standing Long Jump	50-Yard Dash	600-Yard Run/Walk
Age 10	3 to 8 Pull-ups, or a Flexed Arm Hang, to be held 38-50 sec.	35 to 45 in 60 sec.	5'2" to 5'10"	7.7 sec. to 7.4 sec.	2 min. 15 sec. to 2 min.
Age 11	3 to 9 Pull-ups, or a Flexed Arm Hang, to be held 40-50 sec.	38 to 48 in 60 sec.	5'6" to 6'2"	7.6 sec. to 7.2 sec.	2 min. 10 sec. to 1 min. 55 sec.

NOTE: Detailed directions for these test exercises follow.

TEST EXERCISES FOR CHILDREN

Preparing for the   *Correct Flexed Arm*
Flexed Arm Hang   *Hang Position*

Flexed-Arm Hang

Purpose: To measure the strength and endurance of the arms and shoulders.

Equipment: A horizontal bar or piece of pipe about 1¼ to 1½ inches in diameter to be mounted above the youngster's reaching height. The bar should be fixed safely in the basement or outside the home so that the child may practice either flexed-arm hangs or pull-ups.
A stopwatch or a watch with sweep hand for scoring. A low stool, preferably a step stool, so that the child can get into the starting position.

Action: The child grasps the bar. Hands should be about shoulder width apart. The back of hands toward the face. Thumbs under the bar. The child steps off the stool with arms bent, holding chin above the bar, chest close to the bar. The child holds chin above the top edge of the bar as long as possible.

Scoring: Start the watch when the child is hanging with chin above top edge of the bar. Stop watch when the chin either touches the bar or falls below the top edge of the bar. The score is the number of seconds the child holds the Flexed-Arm Hang position.

NOTE: Pull-ups may be done with same equipment. See Physical Aptitude material in Chapter 8 for details.

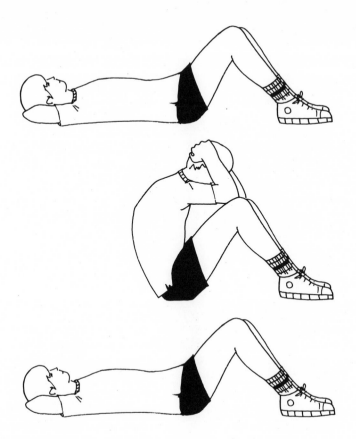

Bent-Leg Situp

Purpose: To measure the strength and endurance of the abdominal muscles.

Equipment: Floor with carpet or exercise mat.
A stopwatch or a watch with sweep hand for scoring.

Action: Have child lie on his back on the floor with knees bent between 45 and 90 degrees. Feet flat on the floor. With someone holding the child's feet in place have the child do as many curls as possible, keeping fingers interlaced behind the head. A repetition is complete when the elbows touch the knees.

Scoring: The score is the number of repetitions completed in one minute.

Start

Takeoff

Landing

Standing Long Jump

Purpose: To measure strength and power of the legs.

Equipment: A tape measure.

Action: Same as for the West Point Physical Aptitude Examination on page 145.

Helpful Hint: When getting ready to jump, have your child swing arms backward and bend knees. In executing jump, have child swing arms forward vigorously as feet leave the ground. Practice is necessary to get coordination correct.

Scoring: Same as for Physical Aptitude Examination, i.e., best of three trials.

Crouch Start

Standing Up Start

50-Yard Dash

Purpose: To measure running speed.

Equipment: Stopwatch and a straight level area.

Action: At the command of "Get set, Go" the child should run 50 yards in a straight line as fast as possible. May use either the stand-up or crouch start.

Scoring: Time to the nearest tenth of a second is the score.

Helpful Hint: Make certain that your child runs with toes pointing straight to the front, as opposed to the splayfoot, when toes are pointed out. Also, note that your child will do better if someone runs alongside at the same time.

600-Yard Run/Walk

Purpose: To measure running endurance.

Equipment: Preferably a running track, but can be any flat, open area where you can measure off 600 yards. A stopwatch or watch with sweep hand.

Action: On the starting commands of "Get set, Go" have your child run/walk 600 yards as fast as possible. Walking is permissible, but the idea is to cover the 600 yards in the least time.

Scoring: The time to the nearest second is the score.

General Rules and Concepts for Parents

No two children are exactly alike or are likely to develop physically and mentally at the same rate.

You cannot force learning until the nervous system is ready for it. For example, no matter how much you work with an infant, he will not walk until his neuromuscular system is ready.

In the preschool years learning is "coincidental." If you insist on practicing throwing every day at a certain time, the child will become bored. Instead, step in with some help when the child is playing with a ball or begin by playing a game that involves throwing, running, or a skill that needs practice.

Begin with simple skills. Don't expect a child to learn to run and throw at the same time.

Remember that no matter how active children are, under the age of 10 they don't have the endurance for long, hard runs or swims. After the age of 10 the progression should be gradual.

Give a child an opportunity to practice skills. Encourage the child to bounce a ball off the side of the house and to climb the jungle gym. Encourage group play because children learn by imitation, especially from children who are one or two years older.

Understand that physical development cannot be separated from emotional, mental, and social development. The development of the total person should always be the ob-

jective of any educational program whether in the home or school. A child shouldn't go to the extreme of spending all or most of his time in physical activity. When necessary, insist that a child eliminate some physical activity to make time for development in other areas.

CHAPTER 8

The Teen Years—12 to 17

As you get older, you will discover that physical fitness is one of your most important personal assets. One benefit of conditioning is an attractive physique, but physical fitness is also the source of energy and stamina, which you can use to meet new challenges and new relationships. Whether you are a boy or girl, here's your first challenge to determine your present state of fitness.

If you think you're already in good condition, flip ahead a few pages and test yourself against the West Point Physical Aptitude Examination. Then see if you can do the Basic Six conditioning exercises for teen-agers at the advanced level. If you pass, congratulations. If not, come on back and finish reading this.

The good news is that we know how to get you looking good and feeling stronger, which means having more energy and vigor. And the sooner you get started, the better. If you put off shaping up until you're pushing 19 or 20, it may be too late. There are things that go along with physical fitness, such as coordination, agility, grace, and game skills, that are better learned early if you want to avoid looking clumsy by the time you're 20.

No other American institution has had more experience in the physical development of teen-agers than West Point. Since 1802 we have tested tens of thousands of applicants to West Point, and we have learned their strengths and weaknesses. For example, we know that in recent years there has been more and more sport specialization among teen-age boys. Many of you are channeling most of your efforts into a single sport. As a result we see applicants with lopsided conditioning: Some muscles are strong, and others are weak.

In preparing for the admission of women cadets we tested

over 3,000 teen-age girls, using the same physical-aptitude examination given male applicants. We didn't expect these women to score as well as men because women on the average are smaller and have less muscle mass. However, we discovered that ordinary, grass-roots sexual bias has been the major factor in cheating women out of the healthy physical development that is available to boys and men.

For generations we have been shunting girls and women over to the sidelines to watch boys and men play games as though physical fitness were a privilege reserved only for men. Discouraging women's participation in sports and conditioning has resulted in depriving teen-age girls of the opportunity to develop the primary muscle groups, which contribute to good health, vigor, and a more attractive appearance.

We took all these factors into consideration. To open West Point's door to women applicants, we modified the requirements on the physical-aptitude tests, and then we began to plan a conditioning program to help women cadets overcome their handicaps. We have now developed what we believe is the best physical fitness program for women in the world, just as we have always tried to maintain the best for men cadets, and it is that expertise that we will share with you.

What's in It for You?

West Point is interested in the whole person: intelligence and therefore academic grades, character and therefore integrity, leadership and therefore a high degree of responsibility, and physical fitness to acquire the strength and endurance to meet all the foregoing criteria.

Years ago we learned that a heavy schedule of sports and military training weren't comprehensive in conditioning the primary muscle groups. And so we designed a personal conditioning program for the cadets. It is taught to them in their first two months, just as you will have the chance to learn it in this book, and then it is the responsibility of each cadet to continue the program on his or her own time. For example, even the varsity football player continues with the personal conditioning program during the football season because he knows that playing any single sport isn't comprehensive in itself.

The teen-age personal conditioning program designed for you

is adapted from the one used by the cadets. It isn't as strenuous as the cadets', but it will still demand work. Is it worth the effort? Check the following and decide for yourself:

The conditioning program is worthwhile

• if you're concerned with your appearance, which means getting rid of fat and flabby muscle

• if you want to improve your sport skills—tennis, swimming, boxing, or whatever—at the varsity or recreational level

• if you want to build up stamina to carry you through the school day with a reserve of energy for an evening of heavy studies or a heavy date

• if you want to apply to West Point

• if you don't want to go to West Point but perhaps someday you'd like to climb a mountain or become a surgeon or a mechanic; in short, if you want to keep your options open until you are absolutely certain of what you want to do with your life

• if you're a girl who has been lucky enough to be a tomboy, because this will help you to maintain your present conditioning

• if you're not a tomboy but you're tired of male chauvinism and paternalism

• if your parents nag at you about your posture and, secretly, you'd like to do something about it

These are some of the reasons you might consider before taking on the program, but there is still another one. The teen period is critical in physical development. If you don't develop some skills and muscles now, you may never be able to catch up.

Sexual Differences in Physical Fitness

Up to the age of puberty, about 12, girls are the equal or a little ahead of boys in physical development. As one grows into adolescence, the advantage goes to the young man.

The young, teen-age male suddenly begins to shoot up; his legs and arms are longer, and he is also "bigger." He is getting that bulky, masculine look. This comes from the rapid growth of muscle. The young man gets help in building muscles from the male sex hormone testosterone.

Now a very different hormone, estrogen, is working in the young female. Estrogen is believed to inhibit the growth of muscle tissue. This does not mean, however, that the young woman can't continue developing strength for tennis, gymnastics, soccer, basketball, or whatever she chooses. All it means is that on a one-to-one basis, a man will have more physiological advantages. The strongest man in the world will be stronger than the strongest woman. So what? Most of us don't want *that* much conditioning. What we do want is enough strength, endurance, agility, and coordination to handle our body weight.

The young woman should realize that until the age of puberty virtually all girls are tomboys in the sense that if she wishes, she is a boy's equal or better. She can run as fast or faster, as far or farther, and if she wishes, hit a ball harder *if* she is encouraged to get out and run and play.

Many girls have been told that any vigorous physical activity is "defeminizing." This is nonsense. There is virtually no possibility of developing bulging muscles, a masculine swagger, or a deep voice. Look at women who swim or play tennis or golf. Are they defeminized? Are they unattractive? Do you know of any woman who is more graceful than a woman gymnast? (See Chapter 14, For Women Only, for information pertinent to women and fitness.)

The young teen-age woman who wants a career will need just as much stamina and muscular endurance to be a surgeon, a pilot or a mechanic as a man will. She will need stamina and endurance in any kind of job to prove that a woman can stand up under pressure as well as a man can. If she chooses the role of housewife and mother, rather than a career outside the home —whoever said that raising children and keeping up a home is easy? In many instances the housewife is working harder physically than the female executive.

It should be obvious to you that we are very concerned about teen-age girls and women. We were disturbed by the findings in our studies. We realize as parents and health professionals that we have been neglecting our young women for generations. Literally, we have been guilty of old-fashioned paternalism and chauvinism. We want that corrected. And we want the best for you.

The best is a balanced conditioning program to insure overall health and fitness, along with game playing to improve agility and coordination. These goals are the same for both teen-age boys and girls.

How Much Conditioning Do You Need?

In designing the conditioning programs for older men and women we have suggested that each adapt the plans to fit his individual needs, depending on his job and leisure-time activities. For teen-agers the advice is different. It is impossible for teen-agers to visualize what their lives will be like in their twenties or thirties, what work they will be doing, what their leisure interests will be, and what sports they will be playing instead of football, baseball, and soccer. And so for teen-agers the advice is to get as much as you can of physical conditioning and academic education in order to keep all of your options open.

How to Get Started

You can begin conditioning by turning to the Teen-Agers' Basic Six plan. Four of the Basic Six exercises condition your body's large muscle groups, and this is important whether you are interested in appearance or athletic skills.

The fifth exercise is for the lower arms, because in our experience we have found that many young men and women have a weak grip which is a handicap in many sports and jobs.

The sixth exercise, Walk/Run, helps develop your cardiorespiratory fitness. This is vital for developing the energy and stamina that eventually separate the boys and girls from the men and women.

If you haven't been doing any exercises, you will want to start at the beginning level for your age group. One principle of conditioning is overload, and it is the quality and amount of exercise that accounts for enough overload, or stress, to develop muscles. The stress is moderate, and increased each week. If you find the level at the first week too easy, then go on to the second week or third or fourth.

For most teen-agers the beginning level should be enough stress for a start. If you then exercise five days each week, the progressive increase in the amount of work is just about right. If you decide to work out only three alternate days a week, then you should stay at each level twice as long. If you find any level difficult, then spend twice as much time or more if necessary at lower levels. For instance, you can spend eight weeks at each of the beginning and intermediate levels and then as much time as is necessary at the advanced level.

The Teen-Agers' Basic Six has deliberately been designed with one set of exercises for both sexes, and why not? Women and men have the same primary muscle groups and the same cardiorespiratory systems. Both should be able to progress at the same rate except for one problem. If a teen-age girl has not been active in sports, she may have fallen behind in conditioning. Therefore, in two categories of exercises—abdomen and shoulder girdle (the muscles of the arms, chest, and shoulders) —you will find two different sets of repetitions. The upper is for girls and the lower for boys. It's recommended, but not necessary, that every young woman eventually works at the boys' level. We are looking at this as a transitional period. Eventually it should not be necessary to have any separate exercises for boys and girls.

How Tough Will It Be?

Will you be able to do the Teen-Agers' Basic Six?

This Basic Six is an adaptation of the West Point conditioning program for cadets. The exercises are demanding, but if they didn't make you work and sweat a little, the program would be a waste of your time. If the exercises are a little difficult in the beginning, work at them.

One of the most important lessons that a new cadet learns at West Point is that he or she has been underestimating his or her capacity for physical and mental work. Another lesson is that he or she cannot shift responsibility. Neither one's muscles nor one's brain will go to work unless one orders them to become active.

Once you've begun the Teen-Ager's Basic Six, you should look at the other components of physical fitness that may take little or none of your time, depending on your present condition.

Weight Control and Nutrition

In Chapter 5, Weight Control and Nutrition, you'll find desirable-weight charts for adults but not for teen-agers. The reason is that the early years of life are growing years. Most youngsters grow in spurts and the spurts may occur at different times. For this reason we cannot generalize about desirable weights in the early years. On the other hand, if you are fat, *you* know it, for you are your own best judge and the most critical.

If you are still uncertain about being fat, undress in front of a mirror. See if the mirror has a message for you. Pinch around your waistline for flab. Lift up your arm and check for loose flesh on the back of the upper arm. Look in the mirror at your buttocks. They should have a good, firm curve and should not droop. Another test is to lie flat on your back. Your abdomen should be concave. If you lay a ruler from your rib cage to your pelvis, the ruler should bridge over your stomach. And this is equally true for both sexes.

You must consult with your physician or the school nurse before beginning a diet. Because of the fast growing in early years and the increased activity during the teens the caloric allowance per day for a teen-ager may differ from that recommended for an adult. Not necessarily, but it may.

When you've decided on your daily allowance of calories, then turn to the diet plan in Chapter 5. The plan is medically sound. It will help you diet without counting calories, and it assures you of a proper food balance.

Flexibility: A Major Component of Physical Fitness

You probably think that only the over-30 set has to worry about flexibility. You're wrong. Flexibility—the ability to bend, stretch, twist, turn, lift, and throw without difficulty—is so important to teen-agers that we begin to test the flexibility of new cadets within 48 hours of their arrival. The reason is that flexibility, the lack of it or the excess of it, can be the cause of accidents and injuries.

In Chapter 4, Flexibility, you'll find simple tests for checking flexibility in different parts of your body. There are exercises that take very little time to help you improve your flexibility if needed. However, if your flexibility is good, then there is something important that you should know:

You can lose flexibility quickly. This happens to young adults when they take jobs that require their sitting a lot. This can also happen to teen-agers who have heavy study schedules or have hobbies or perhaps interests, such as studying piano, that also require a lot of sitting.

Once you lose flexibility, it takes a lot of time to get it back. And you will want it back if you hope to remain limber and agile and want to prevent a lot of backache. The message is simple: If you have good flexibility, then maintain it with a little of the right kind of exercise every day.

Posture—Drag or Sag?

West Point probably knows more about good posture than any other institution in the country. We know that most teen-agers are so pestered by well-meaning parents to "stand straight" that they'd rather talk about something else. We can also estimate that up to 90 percent of the country's teen-agers and parents are misinformed about what is good posture, why you need it, and how you get it.

In the first place, good posture is not walking around like a stick with your shoulder blades pinched back and your head immobilized like a robot's. To the contrary, good posture includes relaxed shoulders and hips, but shoulders and hips in balance. Posture means eliminating stomach and buttock sag, and it means curves only where curves are meant to be. And if you're feeling a little short, good posture will add an inch or more to your height.

When we talk posture at West Point, we are also talking about improvement of your coordination and balance as well as your appearance. And because we know good posture affects a person's outlook on life, we're talking about the kind of pride that comes from self-confidence.

If you decide that you're interested, see Chapter 11. This will tell you how to score your appearance and how to go about correcting any posture problem you may have.

BBC (Beyond Basic Conditioning)

You may find all the conditioning you want in the Teen-Agers' Basic Six. If you want more, Chapter 10, BBC—Beyond Basic Conditioning, will take you into light weights (dumbbells), and either sex can go into this. If you want to go into body building with heavy weights, you must have the personal supervision and programing of a professional along with professional equipment, which is what cadets get who choose this route.

If you aren't interested in increasing your overall muscular strength, you can use BBC selectively to strengthen muscles for your particular sports interest. A chart will direct you to the appropriate exercises.

Two things you should know:

Neither light- nor heavy-weight exercises will make you muscle-bound if you do the exercises correctly and/or if you maintain your flexibility.

Women can do both light- and heavy-weight exercises, and some young women are doing both today, without fear of developing bulging muscles. (See Chapter 14, For Women Only.)

The Ultimate Challenge

At West Point the maintenance of physical fitness is as important as the maintenance of high academic grades. The physical activities range from personal conditioning and military training to 41 different sports or activities, which in turn range from scuba diving through several dozen land-based sports to sky diving. We have a staff of 50 men and women who are professionals in the development of fitness to supervise and train cadets. Yet despite the intensity of physical activity, we know the limits of the cadets when they enter.

For men cadets the West Point Physical Aptitude Examination, page 145, correlates very closely with what we may expect in physical performance. We can make cadets stronger and increase their endurance. We can teach them new physical skills. However, their aptitude will remain at about the same level.

As a teen-ager, in a learning period, you can improve your aptitude for athletics and other physical activities. Test yourself now against the aptitude examination and then come back to it again in six months or a year.

For women cadets the aptitude examination, as we noted, is a compromise based on the knowledge that most women's fitness has been neglected. As a young teen-age woman starting a program at the age of 12 or 13, you should by the time you are 17 be able to do better than the examination for women applicants. In fact, you should be doing pull-ups like the men.

Questions to Be Answered

Q. *Suppose I can't do push-ups, not even one?*

A. Then do modified push-ups until you build enough

strength to do the regular push-up. (See Chapter 2.)

Another suggestion if you can't do even one pull-up is to begin by getting your chin up on the bar with the aid of a stool or with someone holding you, and then let yourself down slowly. We call these "negative pull-ups." We've tried this with 240-pound football linemen who insisted that they could never do pull-ups, and it worked. All teen-agers should be able to lift their body weight.

Q. *Suppose I feel very tired after doing the exercises?*

A. Perhaps you will need a physical checkup, but a bad reaction is usually an indication that you are in very poor condition. If this happens, if you feel sore and very tired, then lay off for about 24 hours, and when you start again, begin with three-quarters or half as many exercises. You should know that moderate exercise very often helps people overcome chronic fatigue.

Q. *Can I stop exercising after I've reached the advanced level?*

A. You can never stop. The body will not store conditioning. Within three days you will begin to lose conditioning. If you lay off for a week or more, you should plan starting up again at a lower level. However, when you've reached the advanced level, you ought to begin enjoying some of that conditioning. Join a dance class. Go backpacking. Take up kayaking. Learn a new game. See Lifetime Sports, Chapter 13, for some ideas.

Q. *How do I monitor my progress?*

A. Turn to Chapter 6, Testing and Recording Your Progress. It will tell you how and when.

Notes on Using the Teen-Agers' Basic Six Progression Chart

1. All exercise sessions should begin with warm-up and cooling-off exercises. See Section I for illustrations and descriptions.

2. The figures in boxes in each chart represent the number of repetitions.

3. In the abdominal and the arms-shoulders-chest categories the top number should be considered the minimum performance level for girls. The bottom number is a goal for all boys but everyone should attempt to reach it.

4. To interpret the progression in the walk/run, you read from the top down. For example, in the first week for ages 12 and 13 in the beginning level you have:

6

220

0. 50

———

1

Interpreted, this means that during the first week six times each day you will run 220 yards in 50 seconds. In between the runs you will spend 1 minute in a slow jog or brisk walk.

5. In all exercising good form is necessary. Quality over quantity is always preferable. You're better off doing an exercise correctly four times rather than sloppily a dozen times. For detailed information on matters ranging from correct breathing and running to how to select proper clothing and shoes, see Chapter 12, Tips for Better Performance.

TEEN-AGERS' BASIC SIX PROGRESSION CHART
(Beginning Level — Four Weeks)

Week	Abdomen — Bent-Knee Half-Curl				Trunk (Waist) — Trunk Twister				Thighs, Hips, Buttocks, Lower Back — Mountain Climber				Arms, Shoulders, Chest — 6-Count Push-up				Lower Arms (Grip) — Towel Squeeze				Cardiorespiratory System — Walk/Run			
	1st	2nd	3rd	4th	1st	2nd	3rd	4th	1st	2nd	3rd	4th	1st	2nd	3rd	4th	1st	2nd	3rd	4th	1st	2nd	3rd	4th
Ages 12 and 13	$\frac{6}{8}$	$\frac{8}{10}$	$\frac{10}{13}$	$\frac{12}{16}$	10	12	14	16	12	14	17	20	$\frac{10}{12}$	$\frac{12}{14}$	$\frac{14}{16}$	$\frac{16}{18}$	30	35	40	50	$6 \times 220\ \frac{0:50}{1}$	$7 \times 220\ \frac{0:50}{1}$	$8 \times 220\ \frac{0:50}{1}$	$8 \times 220\ \frac{0:50}{1}$
Hold each curl 4 sec.																					8.99 mph			
Ages 14 and 15	$\frac{8}{10}$	$\frac{10}{13}$	$\frac{12}{16}$	$\frac{14}{20}$	12	14	16	18	16	19	22	26	$\frac{12}{16}$	$\frac{14}{19}$	$\frac{16}{22}$	$\frac{18}{26}$	30	40	50	60	$6 \times 220\ \frac{0:40}{1}$	$7 \times 220\ \frac{0:40}{1}$	$8 \times 220\ \frac{0:40}{1}$	$9 \times 220\ \frac{0:40}{1}$
Hold each curl 6 sec.																					11.26 mph			
Ages 16 and 17	$\frac{10}{14}$	$\frac{12}{17}$	$\frac{14}{19}$	$\frac{16}{22}$	14	16	18	20	20	24	28	32	$\frac{14}{18}$	$\frac{16}{22}$	$\frac{18}{26}$	$\frac{20}{30}$	30	40	50	60	$8 \times 220\ \frac{0:40}{1}$	$9 \times 220\ \frac{0:40}{1}$	$10 \times 220\ \frac{0:40}{1}$	$11 \times 220\ \frac{0:40}{1}$
Hold each curl 8 sec.																					11.26 mph			

TEEN-AGERS' BEGINNING LEVEL
Category: **Abdomen**

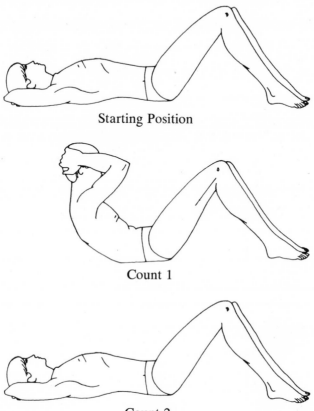

Starting Position

Count 1

Count 2

Bent-Knee Half-Curl

Starting Position: Lie on back with knees bent in a 45- to 90-degree angle. Feet together on floor. Hands interlaced behind your head.

Action: Count 1. Begin by tucking your chin against your chest. Then curl forward slowly until you are in the half-curl position. Hold that position for the time prescribed in the progression chart.

          Count 2. Slowly return to the starting position.

Cadence: Slow.

Category: **Trunk (Waist)**

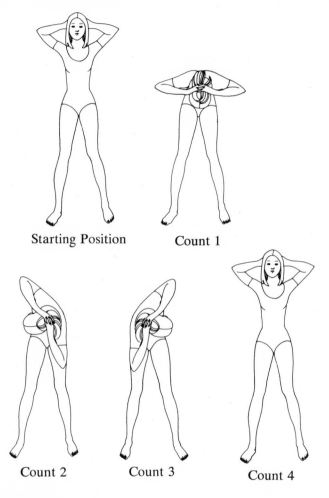

Starting Position   Count 1

Count 2   Count 3   Count 4

Trunk Twister

Starting Position: Stand with feet separated about shoulder width.
Hands interlaced behind your head. Elbows back.

Action: Count 1. Bend forward at the waist, keeping knees
straight.

Count 2. Twist trunk to the left, keeping elbows back.

Count 3. Twist trunk to the right, keeping elbows
back.

Count 4. Return to the starting position.

Cadence: Moderate. Gradually increase the force of the twists.

Category: **Thighs, Hips, Buttocks, Lower Back**

Starting Position

Count 1

Count 2

Mountain Climber

Starting Position: Squat with hands on the floor and left leg extended to the rear. The right knee will be inside the right elbow.

Action: Count 1. In the same motion reverse the position of the feet, bringing the left foot under the body and extending the right leg backward.

Count 2. Reverse the feet again, returning to the starting position.

Cadence: Start out at moderate pace and switch to fast pace.

Category: **Arms, Shoulders, Chest**

Starting Position

Count 1

Count 2

Count 3

Count 4

Count 5

Count 6

Six-Count Push-up

Starting Position: Stand with head up. Arms at sides. Feet together.

Action: Count 1. Squat down placing palms flat on the floor
at about shoulder width apart, arms inside
the knees.

Count 2. Thrust legs backward into front-leaning rest
position as in illustration. Keep back and
legs straight.

Count 3. Continuing to keep back and legs straight,
bend arms at elbow until your chest touches
floor.

Count 4. Straighten arms and return to front-leaning
rest position.

Count 5. Return to squatting position.

Count 6. Return to starting position.

Cadence: Moderate.

Category: **Lower Arms (Grip)**

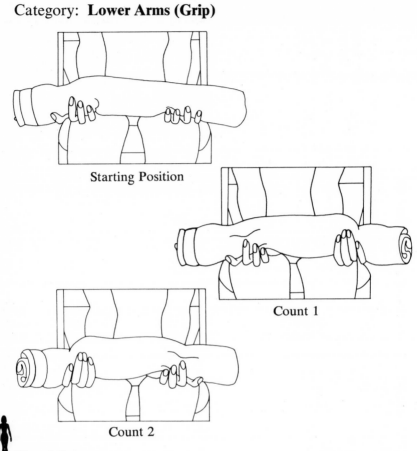

Starting Position

Count 1

Count 2

Towel Squeeze

Starting Position: (Begin by preparing a long bath towel for the exercise. Fold the towel in quarters and then roll it into a cylinder. The thickness of the cylinder should be small enough to get your hand around it when you squeeze.) Hold the towel in both hands with palms facing up.

Action: Count 1. Grasp the towel with your left hand, tightening your hand as much as possible. Hold for two seconds and then release.

Count 2. Follow the same procedure with right hand.

Cadence: Slow.

NOTE: A small sponge-rubber ball or a commercial handgrip exercise may be used instead of the towel.

TEEN-AGERS' BASIC SIX PROGRESSION CHART
(Intermediate Level — Four Weeks)

Week	Abdomen Bent-Knee Curl				Trunk (Waist) Full Twister				Thighs, Hips, Buttocks, Lower Back — Chair or Chair Step				Arms, Shoulders, Chest — 8-Count Push-up				Lower Arms (Grip) — Wrist Roller				Cardiorespiratory System — Walk/Run			
	1st	2nd	3rd	4th	1st	2nd	3rd	4th	1st	2nd	3rd	4th	1st	2nd	3rd	4th	1st	2nd	3rd	4th	1st	2nd	3rd	4th
Ages 12 and 13	20/25	25/30	30/35	35/40	10	12	14	16	1	1½	2	2½ (Minutes)	8/10	10/12	12/14	14/16	6	8	10	12 (With 5 lb. of weight)	3 x 440, 1:45/2	4 x 440, 1:45/2	5 x 440, 1:45/2	6 x 440, 1:45/2 — 8.56 mph
Ages 14 and 15	25/35	30/40	35/45	40/50	12	14	16	18	2	2½	3	4 (Minutes)	10/14	12/14	14/18	16/20	6	8	10	12 (With 8 lb. of weight)	3 x 440, 1:30/2	4 x 440, 1:30/2	5 x 440, 1:30/2	6 x 440, 1:30/2 — 10 mph
Ages 16 and 17	30/45	35/50	40/55	45/60	14	16	18	20	3	4	5	5 (Minutes)	12/16	14/18	16/20	18/22	8	10	12	14 (With 10 lb. of weight)	4 x 440, 1:25/2	5 x 440, 1:25/2	6 x 440, 1:25/2	7 x 440, 1:25/2 — 10.59 mph

TEEN-AGERS' INTERMEDIATE LEVEL
Category: **Abdomen**

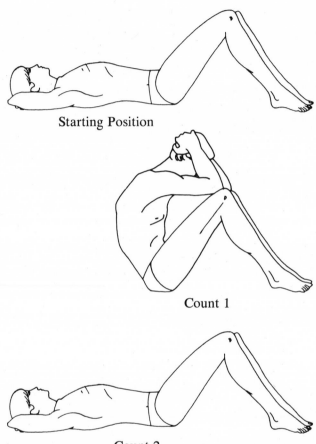

Starting Position

Count 1

Count 2

Bent-Knee Curl

Starting Position: Lie on back with knees bent in an angle of 45 to 90 degrees. Hands interlaced behind head.

Action: Count 1. Tucking chin into chest, curl forward slowly into a sitting position until you can touch your elbows to your knees.

Count 2. Return to the starting position.

Cadence: Start this exercise slowly and gradually increase the pace.

Category: **Trunk (Waist)**

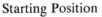

Starting Position	Count 1	Count 2

Count 3	Count 4	Count 5

Full Twister

Starting Position: Stand with feet separated about shoulder width. Hands on hips.

Action: Count 1. Bend forward from waist as far as possible.

Count 2. Moving in a circular pattern from the waist, move your trunk to the left.

Count 3. Continue to circle in the same direction until you are bending backward from the waist.

Count 4. Continue to circle trunk to the right side.

Count 5. Return to the starting position.

Cadence: Slow.

Category: **Thighs, Hips, Buttocks, Lower Back**

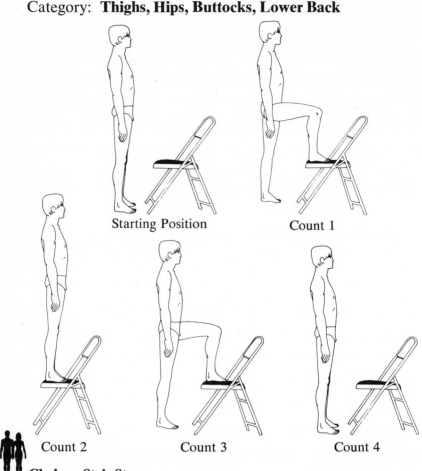

Starting Position

Count 1

Count 2

Count 3

Count 4

Chair or Stair Step

Starting Position: (Use a sturdy chair, stool, or bench between 15 to 17 inches high. Or the second step of a stairway, if it is 15 to 17 inches off the floor.) Stand head up, arms at sides, facing chair or stairs.

Action: Count 1. Place the right foot on the chair or the second step of the stairs.

Count 2. Bring the left foot up beside the right foot and stand straight.

Count 3. Lower the right foot to the floor.

Count 4. Lower the left foot to the floor.

Cadence: Moderate to fast pace. Try to complete one full repetition every two seconds.

Category: **Arms, Shoulders, Chest**

Count 1

Count 2

Starting
Position

Count 3

Count 4

Count 5

Count 6

Count 7

Count 8

Eight-Count Push-up

Starting Position: Stand with feet together. Arms at sides.
    Head up.

Action: Count 1. Squat down. Place palms flat on floor about
        shoulder width apart. Arms inside knees.
        Count 2. Thrust legs backward into front-leaning po-
        sition.
        Count 3. Bend arms, lowering body until chest touches
        floor. Keep legs and body straight.
        Count 4. Raise to front-leaning position.
        Count 5. Again touch chest to floor.
        Count 6. Raise to front-leaning position.
        Count 7. Return to squatting position.
        Count 8. Return to starting position.

Cadence: Moderate.

Category: **Lower Arms (Grip)**

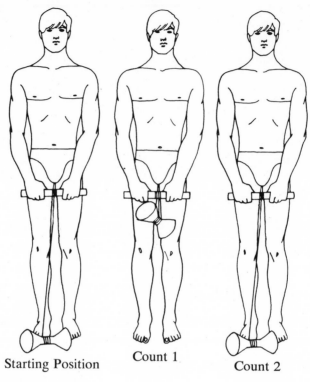

Starting Position   Count 1   Count 2

Wrist Roller

Starting Position: (Prepare the wrist roller by getting a round stick 15 to 18 inches long and about the thickness of a large broomstick. Attach a clothesline rope 4 to 5 feet long to the stick with a nail or by drilling hole through stick. Tie other end of rope to dumbbell.) Stand with feet separated shoulder width. Arms at sides with palms down holding the handle of the wrist roller.

Action: Count 1. Wind rope up on handle.
Count 2. Slowly unwind rope.
Count 3. Repeat Count 1 with palms facing up.
Count 4. Repeat Count 2 with palms facing up.

Cadence: Slow.

NOTE: A longer rope can be used for this exercise if you are standing on a bench or sturdy chair.

TEEN-AGERS' BASIC SIX PROGRESSION CHART
(Advanced Level — Four Weeks)

Week	Abdomen — Isolated Curl				Trunk (Waist) — Body Twist				Thighs, Hips, Buttocks, Lower Back — Flutter Kick				Arms, Shoulders, Chest — Classic Push-up				Lower Arms (Grip) — Wrist Roller				Cardiorespiratory System — Walk/Run				
	1st	2nd	3rd	4th	1st	2nd	3rd	4th	1st	2nd	3rd	4th	1st	2nd	3rd	4th	1st	2nd	3rd	4th	1st	2nd	3rd	4th	
Ages 12 and 13	$\frac{10}{12}$	$\frac{12}{15}$	$\frac{14}{18}$	$\frac{16}{20}$	10	12	14	16	20	25	30	35	$\frac{14}{16}$	$\frac{16}{20}$	$\frac{18}{24}$	$\frac{20}{28}$	6	8	10	12 (With 8 lb. of weight)	$\frac{4:00}{3}$ 2 x 880	$\frac{4:00}{3}$ 2 x 880	$\frac{4:00}{3}$ 4 x 880	$\frac{4:00}{2}$ 4 x 880	7.5 mph
Ages 14 and 15	$\frac{12}{18}$	$\frac{14}{20}$	$\frac{16}{23}$	$\frac{18}{25}$	12	14	16	18	30	35	40	50	$\frac{16}{20}$	$\frac{18}{25}$	$\frac{20}{30}$	$\frac{24}{35}$	8	10	12	14 (With 10 lb. of weight)	$\frac{3:30}{3}$ 3 x 880	$\frac{3:30}{3}$ 4 x 880	$\frac{3:30}{3}$ 5 x 880	$\frac{3:30}{3}$ 6 x 880	8.58 mph
Ages 16 and 17	$\frac{14}{22}$	$\frac{16}{25}$	$\frac{18}{28}$	$\frac{20}{30}$	14	16	18	20	40	45	50	60	$\frac{18}{30}$	$\frac{22}{35}$	$\frac{26}{40}$	$\frac{30}{45}$	8	10	12	14 (With 13 lb. of weight)	$\frac{3:20}{3}$ 4 x 880	$\frac{3:20}{3}$ 4 x 880	$\frac{3:20}{3}$ 6 x 880	$\frac{3:20}{3}$ 7 x 880	9.0 mph

TEEN-AGERS' ADVANCED LEVEL
Category: **Abdomen**

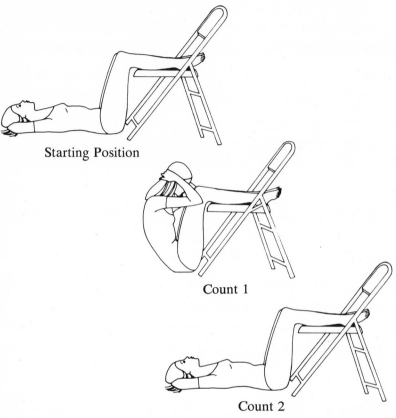

Starting Position

Count 1

Count 2

Isolated Curl

Starting Position: Lie on back. Knees bent. Feet and lower legs resting on chair. Hands interlaced behind head.

Action: Count 1. Tucking chin into chest, curl forward slowly into sitting position until you can touch your elbows to your knees.

Count 2. Return to the starting position.

Cadence: Slow.

NOTE: If you can't do this exercise immediately, then build up to it by starting out with your arms extended over your head and swinging your arms forward as you sit up. You can increase stress by moving hips closer to chair, decrease stress by sliding hips away from chair.

Category: **Trunk (Waist)**

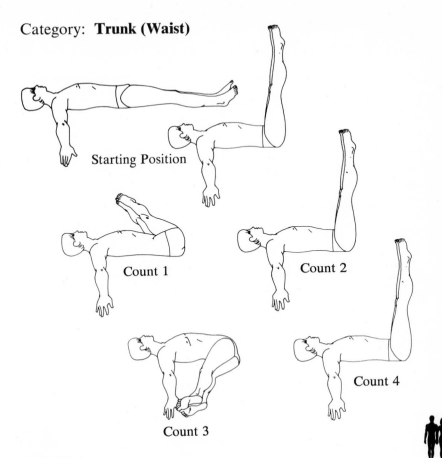

Starting Position

Count 1

Count 2

Count 3

Count 4

Body Twist

Starting Position: Lie on your back with arms extended straight out from shoulders and palms on the floor. Raise legs upward to vertical position, feet together, knees straight.

Action: Count 1. Lower legs to the left, touching floor with feet close to the left hand. At all times keep knees straight and both shoulders on the floor.

Count 2. Return to starting position.

Count 3. Lower legs to the right, touching floor with feet close to the right hand. Again, keep knees straight and both shoulders on floor.

Count 4. Return legs to starting position.

Cadence: Slow.

Category: **Thighs, Hips, Buttocks, Lower Back**

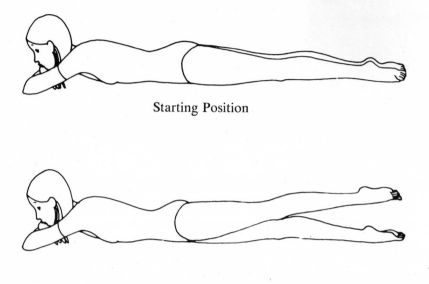

Starting Position

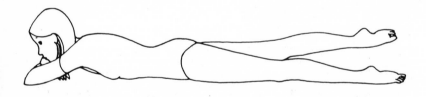

Flutter Kick

Starting Position: Lie face down, hands folded under the chin. Arch the back up, bringing feet off the floor.

Action: Keeping legs fairly straight, kick from the hips, legs alternating, eight to ten inches off the floor. Count each time the left foot comes down as one repetition.

Cadence: Moderate.

Category: **Arms, Shoulders, Chest**

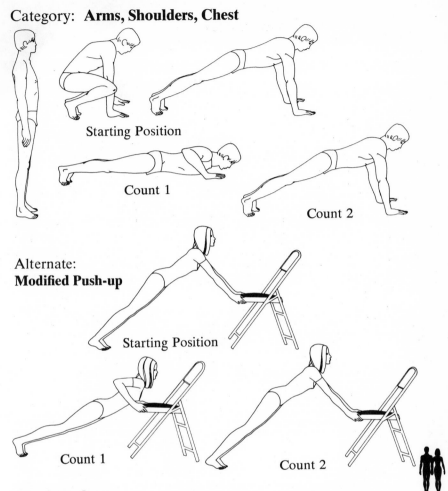

Starting Position

Count 1

Count 2

Alternate:
Modified Push-up

Starting Position

Count 1

Count 2

Classic Push-up

Starting Position: With feet together squat down and place palms flat on floor. Hands should be about shoulder width apart and inside knees. Thrust legs backward into the front-leaning rest position as illustrated.

Action: Count 1. Keeping legs and body straight, bend at elbows until chest touches floor.

Count 2. Straighten arms, returning to starting position.

Cadence: Moderate.

NOTE: If unable to do this type of push-up initially, do the modified push-up.

Category: **Lower Arms (Grip)**

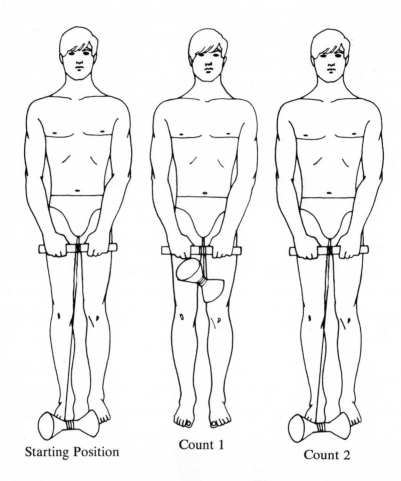

Starting Position   Count 1   Count 2

**Wrist Roller**

Same as in the intermediate level (page 138).

THE WEST POINT PHYSICAL APTITUDE EXAMINATION

All men and women candidates for West Point must pass a physical-aptitude examination to qualify for admission. The examination includes only four items:

1. The standing long jump
2. The modified basketball throw
3. The 300-yard shuttle run
4. Pull-ups for men, flexed-arm hang for women

Can you pass the West Point PAE? Well, give it a try. Be certain to follow the instructions carefully in order that you get valid results. You will need a friend, teacher, or parent to administer the examination. All of these tests should be completed during one testing period.

You will need the following equipment:

1. Pull-up bar
2. Stopwatch
3. Tape measure
4. Basketball
5. A mat to kneel on when you throw the basketball

Standing Long Jump

The jumping area should preferably be marked off on a gymnasium floor. Mark the floor with a takeoff line. If possible, dust the takeoff and jumping area with a very light coat of powdered rosin to prevent slipping. You may also step on a wet towel or rag to increase traction at the takeoff area. Now for the test.

Stand at the starting position with your feet immediately behind the take-off line. You may bend your knees and swing your arms one or more times in order to help you jump forward the greatest distance possible.

You must take off with both feet simultaneously and land on both feet simultaneously with the heels approximately even. You are not permitted a preliminary hop.

To score, measure the distance from the rear edge of the takeoff line to the back of the rearmost heel on landing. You get to do three correctly executed jumps. The best jump is the one that counts.

NOTE: If you land flat-footed after the jump, you are allowed to fall forward but not backward. If you fall backward, you are allowed another trial.

Modified Basketball Throw

A gymnasium is preferable with a ceiling that is at least 22 feet high. A throwing line is marked at one end of the gym. A mat about five feet wide and two inches thick is placed with one edge even with the rear edge of the throwing line.

The modified basketball throw requires that you get down on your knees on the mat, close and directly behind the throwing line. Your knees must be parallel to the throwing line. You are allowed three legal overhand throws and may use your non-throwing hand to steady the ball in preparation for the throw. You cannot touch on or over the throwing line during or after any throw. You should try to throw the ball down a corridor that is about two to four feet wide. However, the scoring distance will be measured to the point of impact if the ball lands outside the corridor. If the ball hits the ceiling or a side wall, it will not be scored and will be rethrown. All three valid throws are recorded, and the best of the three is the one that counts.

300-Yard Shuttle Run

The running course will be 3 feet wide and 25 yards long, laid out in a straight line. There should be at least 30 feet of unobstructed floor space beyond each end line.

You may start the course from a sprint, crouch, or stand-up start, with both feet behind the starting line. You run six complete round trips for a total of 300 yards. Each time you turn, you must place at least one foot on or over the line. Do not take a circular path to make any turn. Whoever is running the test should advise you of the number of round trips remaining so that on the final trip you may sprint past the finish line. The stopwatch must measure to a tenth of a second.

The commands used are "On your mark, get set, Go." The stopwatch is started exactly on the word *Go* and stopped exactly as your chest crosses the finish line after the sixth round trip. You are scored on only one correctly executed trial.

Pull-ups (Men)

A horizontal bar 1¼ inches in diameter is set at a height of at least eight feet from the floor and at least six feet from any obstacle, such as a wall. The bar should be fixed and stable. It is advisable to clean the bar with towels and sandpaper if necessary. You may use chalk to dry your hands, and you may have a mat on the floor beneath the bar.

You jump to grasp the bar. The back of your hands must be toward your face, and your thumbs must be under the bar. Start from a momentary pause in a straight-arm hang with elbows locked. At the command of "Go" you pull your body upward until your chin is lifted over the bar without tilting your head backward. Then return to the straight-arm-hang position with elbows locked. Repeat the pull-up as many times as possible. That is your score. Only one trial is allowed.

The following precautions must be followed in the pull-ups. You must start from a momentary straight-arm hang. Your chin must be raised over the top of the bar, the bar directly under the chin while your head is held level. Your body must lower to the straight-arm hang on each movement. No kicking or swinging up is permitted. If you start swinging, the tester should extend an arm to stop the swinging and then quickly withdraw to allow you to continue. The cadence should be moderate.

Flexed-Arm Hang (Women)

A horizontal bar similar to the one for pull-ups should be adjusted so that it is approximately equal to your standing height. If this isn't possible, use a stool or two assistants to lift you.

Grasp the bar with your hands approximately shoulder width apart. The back of your hands are toward your face and your thumbs are under the bar.

Two assistants grasp your knees and raise you until your chin is level and above the bar. This is the flexed-arm-hang position. Your elbows are flexed and your chest close to the bar.

At the command "Go" the stopwatch is started, and simultaneously the assistants release your knees. You hold the flexed-arm position as long as possible.

The watch is stopped if your chin falls below the level of the bar, if your head tilts backward to keep your chin above the bar, or if your chin rests on the bar. (NOTE: If your chin inadvertently touches the bar but does not rest on it, the test will continue.) Only one trial is allowed unless unusual circumstances arise, such as your hand slipping due to perspiration or a misunderstanding of your assistants.

Comparing Your Scores

To compare your scores with those of young women and men recently entering West Point, use the following tables:

Average Scores for Men

Standing long jump	7'8"
Modified basketball throw	69'
300-yard shuttle run	59.5 sec.
Pull-ups	9

Passing Scores for Men

Standing long jump	7'1"
Modified basketball throw	61'
300-yard shuttle run	62.5 sec.
Pull-ups	6

Here's something to really shoot at!

Maximum Scores for Men

Standing long jump	9'6"
Modified basketball throw	97'
300-yard shuttle run	50.5 sec.
Pull-ups	20

The above maximum scores indicate what you would have to do in each test in order to obtain a maximum PAE score of 800. Actually, some cadets did better than the scores shown above on individual items.

Average Scores for Women

Standing long jump	6'3"
Modified basketball throw	41'
300-yard shuttle run	66.6 sec.
Flexed-arm hang	30 sec.

Any young man or woman interested in obtaining further details about West Point's admission qualifications, including medical and academic standards, should write for a West Point catalog. Address your request to

Office of the Director of Admissions and Registrar
United States Military Academy
West Point, N.Y. 10996

Men and women are admitted as cadets from the age of 17 to 22, but it's suggested that you write for a catalog as early as your junior year in high school.

CHAPTER 9

The Later Years

Warning: Children May Be Dangerous to Your Health

When men and women get into their late fifties and early sixties, and especially when they become retirees, they need protection from their children, for most children think their parents should take it easy, settle into comfortable rocking chairs (preferably motorized), and just sit there, hum, and look happy.

Children worry about their parents bending, stretching, reaching, and even walking. When your children come visiting, it's to take you for a ride, not for a walk. Somehow young Americans have come to believe that the later years should be indolent, dreamy years when parents take on a golden glow like bronzed baby shoes.

We are talking about children with the best intentions, who pamper you, who are solicitous and considerate, and who more than anything else want you to *take it easy*. Unfortunately, taking it easy, the gift of inactivity, is one of the worst things that can happen to you.

In recent years we've learned a lot about the process of aging. We know that aging is a very gradual, slow process that begins in the early twenties, but anyone can speed it up. A young person who is obese and sedentary literally may look and act middle-aged. On the other hand, there are the men and women who lead vigorous lives into their fifties, sixties and seventies, but when they retire and "take it easy," they deteriorate rapidly.

Keep Moving

What we are scientifically certain of is that no one need age rapidly. You don't have to deteriorate suddenly. You can be

150

mentally and physically active as long as you wish. If you have habitually been playing chess or running several miles a day, or both, you don't have to stop because you are 60, 70, or 80. The secret is to keep active, keep moving, because the active life is not guaranteed. You have to work for it, just as you had to work to have the money to retire. And with retirement you don't change automatically into elderly Barbie dolls.

In our later years we maintain the same personal interests, attitudes, and characteristics. Whatever we've liked—sports, political discussions, books, museums, bowling, jazz, opera, fishing, boating—we will still have the same interests. And many people look forward to retirement because it means having more time to do the things they prefer to do. For most people, retirement should be a time of increased activity, now that you're no longer chained to that desk and chair.

You need resources to enjoy retirement, and one of these resources must be physical fitness. If you have been physically active throughout your life, you are better off, but if you have been sedentary, then you will have to get to work. Both groups, sedentary or active, need to exercise, either to improve or to maintain fitness. Your health in later years can no more be neglected than can your bank account.

Get Moving

You can improve your fitness any time, before the age of 6 or after the age of 60. The extent of your improvement depends on the amount and kind of conditioning you do. If you follow the conditioning plans in this manual, you should know what benefits you may expect.

You will feel better physically:

• The organs of the body, including the digestive organs, will be stimulated through activity and will work better.

• You'll slow down the aging process, which means you'll have better flexibility, balance, and coordination.

• You'll decrease the problem of muscular aches and pain.

• You'll have better control of your body, which will help prevent getting involved in accidents. And there are profound psychological advantages:

• You'll look good. Your new vigor and enjoyment will pick up your spirits.

• Being physically fit, you will have more physical courage, and you'll be more likely to participate in new and stimulating experiences.

• And perhaps most important, you will have your independence. You'll be able to bend, walk, lift, stretch, and run if you wish. As a result you will not be dependent on anyone. You won't have to wait for anyone to help you, and so you will have your self-respect and freedom of action.

What Kind of Conditioning?

The Basic Six, a conditioning program for later years, is progressive, comprehensive, and safe. You start at a beginning level, which assumes that you have been getting little exercise, and gradually work up to a maintenance level. The fitness components include those for other age groups—muscular strength and endurance, cardiorespiratory efficiency, flexibility, and weight control—plus an additional component, balance. However, the priority shifts from development to maintenance of certain of the components.

First priority goes to cardiorespiratory efficiency. It is this component that is involved in the health and function of the heart, lungs and blood vessels. And it is this component which all other organs of the body depend on for survival.

Cardiorespiratory fitness can be developed and maintained at any age. To do this we depend on the large muscle groups, especially those in the legs. Leg muscles are so important to circulation that they are often called the secondary pump. Each time leg muscles contract, they squeeze the large veins of the legs, which forces the blood back to the heart and helps keep circulation at an effective rate. This is particularly important because blood in the lower torso and legs is being returned to the heart against the pull of gravity.

Walking and running are the best kinds of exercises to condition the cardiorespiratory system. Almost as good are cycling and swimming. The Basic Six plan that follows includes an indoor walk/run exercise. For an outdoor plan for men and women up to age 70, see Chapter 3, The Walk/Run Plan.

In later years second priority goes to *flexibility*, which means keeping your body limber and elastic so that you can bend, turn, twist and walk without "creaking" and soreness. Flexibility literally means the ability to move the joints through their normal range of motion. Being able to do this depends primarily on the suppleness of muscle, tendons, ligaments, and other tissue that attach to the joints. This manual contains a special chapter on flexibility for younger age groups. You may use the tests in that section to measure your progress but your flexibility exercises are included in the Basic Six in this chapter.

Another component often neglected in later years is *balance*. Balance degenerates with disuse, and so at each level of body conditioning there is one exercise to help you regenerate and maintain your sense of balance.

Muscular strength and endurance are as important in later years as at any other time in our lives. For example, it is only well-toned muscles that keep gravity from bending older people into a hairpin. And, of course, there's no reason why you shouldn't maintain muscular strength to play golf, sail, tennis, handball, or whatever game you enjoy. Perhaps, as you get into your seventies and eighties, you may not be able to play as long, but you can still have your game and a good one. It's true that muscular strength decreases as we get older because of the loss of muscle tissue, but this is a very slow and gradual decrease. Remember that conditioning exercises as well as the game itself slow down the aging process.

The last major component is *weight control and nutrition*. Most people in their later years have the wisdom to understand the risks of obesity. If you need help in weight control, you'll find the West Point diet as much concerned with nutrition as losing fat. The diet is medically sound, but it's always best to check with your physician before starting any weight-loss plan.

Some Questions About the Basic Six

Q. *Why are these "either sex" exercises?*

A. The exercises work equally well for men and women. A couple can exercise together or with a group of friends. This sometimes makes it easier to maintain frequency and regularity.

Q. *Suppose I can't keep up with my spouse or friends?*

A. It's not important because the conditioning plan is not a game and not competitive. The Basic Six is a personal conditioning plan, which means that you should work at your own rate. If you don't feel strong enough to increase repetitions each week, then stay at the same level for an extra week—or two weeks.

Q. *How long will the program take?*

A. There are three levels with 4 weeks allowed for each level. That adds up to 12 weeks if you work out at least five days of each week. If you work less, you will have to allow twice as much time at each level.

Q. *Suppose I find the program too easy?*

A. You could start out at the intermediate level, but first be certain that you can do all the exercises at the end of the beginning level. Only then will you know for certain that you have the requisite balance and flexibility before going on.

If you reach the end of the maintenance level and it's not challenging enough, then you have several options: You may (1) increase the number of repetitions of each exercise, (2) switch to the beginning level of the 18–50 year group, or (3) go on to BBC. Whatever your decision, be sure to continue your balance and flexibility exercises.

Q. *I think exercises are a bore. Why can't I just play golf or tennis a little more often?*

A. In later years an exercise program is critical to fitness and health, and it is the exercises that will give you the strength and vigor to enjoy sports. No sport replaces the exercises in comprehensive conditioning. It is not either-or. It should preferably be both: exercises for health and fitness, sports for pleasure.

Q. *How will I know if I'm making progress with the Basic Six plan?*

A. You can use the same measurement and record-keeping methods as other age groups which you will find in Chapter 6, Testing and Recording Your Progress.

Q. *How frequently must I exercise once I've reached the maintenance level?*

A. Exercise at least three, but preferably five, times a week. However, if you stop exercising for a time because of illness or an accident, then start up again at a lower level and work up again to the maintenance level. (See Chapter 12, Tips for Better Performance, for information about selecting the proper clothing and shoes, details on correct breathing, running, etc. Women should refer to Chapter 14, For Women Only, for information especially pertinent to women and fitness.)

THE BASIC SIX

Warm-up

Before doing the Basic Six, walk briskly in place or around the room for two minutes. After walking, allow body to slump, crouching as low as possible; then gradually straighten up, stretching to full height and extending arms over head. Repeat this exercise slowly for one minute—about 15 times.

Cooling Off

After doing the Basic Six, continue walking at a slower pace until your heart rate and breathing has slowed to about normal.

BEGINNING LEVEL
Category: **Abdomen**

Starting Position

Count 1

Count 2

Bent-Knee Half-Curl

Starting Position: Lie on back. Heels on floor. Knees bent at a 45- to 90-degree angle. Hands interlaced behind head.

Action: Count 1. Tucking chin into your chest, slowly curl forward until your shoulders are about ten inches off the floor, or as far as you can go.

Hold position off floor for count of two seconds.

Count 2. Slowly return to starting position.

Cadence: Slow.

Repetitions: First week: 3
Second week: 4
Third week: 5
Fourth week: 6

NOTE: If you are unable to raise your body to the curl position, then begin in the sitting position and lower your upper body to the curl position. Hold the curl position for the prescribed count. You should gradually gain enough strength to do the exercise from the lying position.

Category: **Trunk (Waist/Lower Back)**

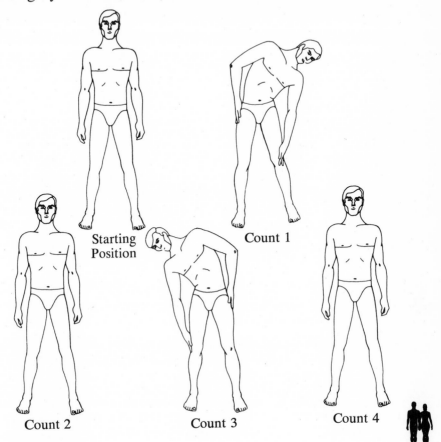

Starting Position

Count 1

Count 2

Count 3

Count 4

Body Bender

Starting Position: Stand with feet shoulder width apart. Arms at sides.

Action: Count 1. Bend trunk sideward to left as far as possible.
Count 2. Return to starting position.
Count 3. Bend trunk to right as far as possible.
Count 4. Return to starting position.

Cadence: Moderate.

Repetitions: First week: 3
Second week: 4
Third week: 5
Fourth week: 6

Category: **Balance**

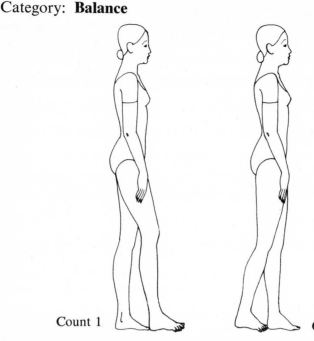

Count 1   Count 2

Heel-to-Toe Walk

Starting Position: Stand up straight (good posture) with left foot
along a straight line. You may hold your arms out
to help keep your balance.

Action: Count 1. Walk along straight line, putting the right
foot in front of the left foot with the right
heel touching the left toe. Continue alternating one foot in front of the other for
number of steps specified below. Count a
step each time the left foot touches the
floor.

Count 2. Return along the line to starting position
by walking backward, toe to heel.

Cadence: Slow.

Repetitions: First week: 5 steps
Second week: 6 steps
Third week: 7 steps
Fourth week: 8 steps

NOTE: If you are uncertain of your balance, you may want to have
someone beside you when you are doing the balance exercise.

Category: **Hips, Thighs, Buttocks**

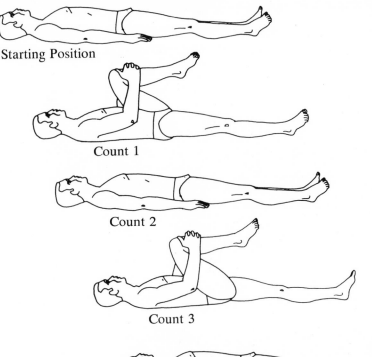

Starting Position

Count 1

Count 2

Count 3

Count 4

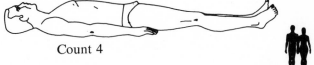

Knee Press

Starting Position: Lie on back, legs extended, feet together, arms along sides.

Action: Count 1. Bend left knee, raising foot off the floor. At same time clasp your knee with both hands and pull slowly toward the chest.
Count 2. Return left leg to starting position.
Count 3. Repeat Count 1, using the right leg.
Count 4. Return to starting position.

Cadence: Slow.

Repetitions: First week: 3
Second week: 4
Third week: 5
Fourth week: 6

Category: **Neck, Arms, Shoulders**

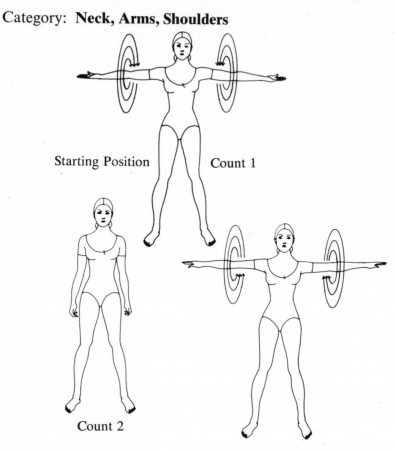

Starting Position   Count 1

Count 2

Arm Circles

Starting Position: Stand with feet separated shoulder width. Head up; buttocks and stomach tucked in. Arms extended out from shoulders parallel to floor.

Action: Count 1. With palms up, rotate arms backward the prescribed number of times.
Count 2. Drop arms to side and relax.
Repeat exercise with forward rotation, palms of hand turned down.

Cadence: Slow and increase to moderate.

Repetitions: First week: 5 each direction
Second week: 6 each direction
Third week: 7 each direction
Fourth week: 8 each direction

Category: **Cardiorespiratory System**

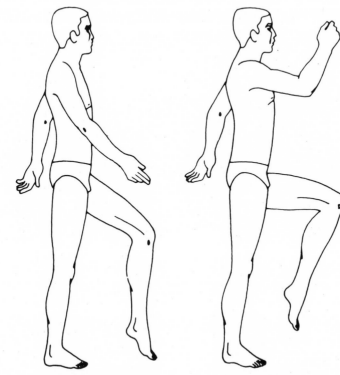

Walk-in-Place   *Run-in-Place*

Walk/Run-in-Place

Starting Position: Stand at attention.

Action for Walk-in-Place: Walk vigorously with toes pointed forward. As endurance builds, increase speed and raise knees higher.

Action for Run-in-place: Run on toes, raising feet four to six inches off the floor. As endurance builds, increase speed and raise knees higher.

Repetitions: Throughout the beginning level, walk/run in place or around the room for two or three minutes. Walk 45 steps, run 15 steps.

NOTE: Walk/run on carpeted or padded floor. Wear tennis or running shoes.

INTERMEDIATE LEVEL
Category: **Abdomen**

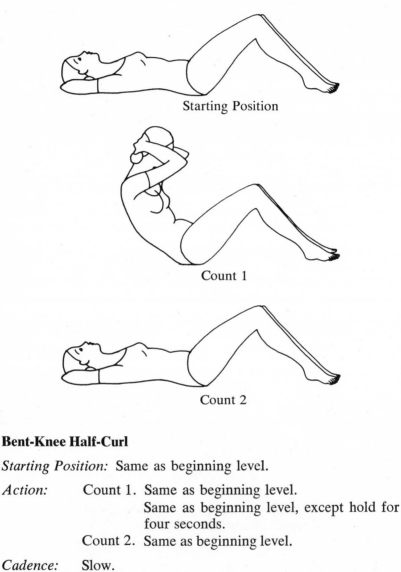

Starting Position

Count 1

Count 2

Bent-Knee Half-Curl

Starting Position: Same as beginning level.

Action: Count 1. Same as beginning level.
                         Same as beginning level, except hold for
                         four seconds.
               Count 2. Same as beginning level.

Cadence: Slow.

Repetitions: First week: 6
               Second week: 6
               Third week: 7
               Fourth week: 7

Category: **Trunk (Waist/Lower Back)**

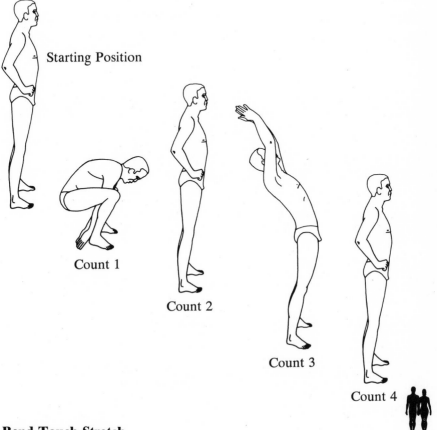

Starting Position

Count 1

Count 2

Count 3

Count 4

Bend-Touch-Stretch

Starting Position: Stand with hands on hips. Feet separated about shoulder width.

Action: Count 1. Bend forward from waist with knees slightly bent and touch the floor.
Count 2. Return to the starting position.
Count 3. Bend backward and stretch.
Count 4. Return to the starting position.

Cadence: Slow.

Repetitions: First week: 5
Second week: 6
Third week: 8
Fourth week: 10

Category: **Balance**

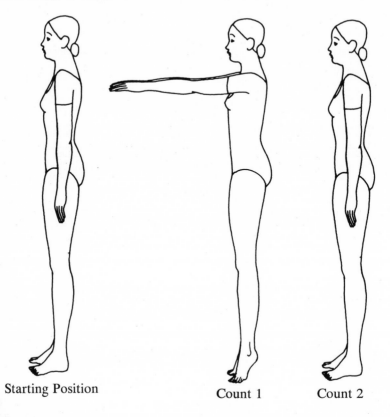

Starting Position   Count 1   Count 2

Toe Stand

Starting Position: Stand with feet separated about six inches. Arms at sides.

Action: Count 1. Rise on toes and swing arms forward and up to shoulder height parallel to the floor. Hold and count slowly to five.

               Count 2. Return to starting position.

Cadence: Slow.

Repetitions: First week: 5
               Second week: 6
               Third week: 7
               Fourth week: 8

NOTE: Do some of the Toe Stand exercises with your eyes open and some with your eyes closed.

Category: **Hips, Thighs, Buttocks**

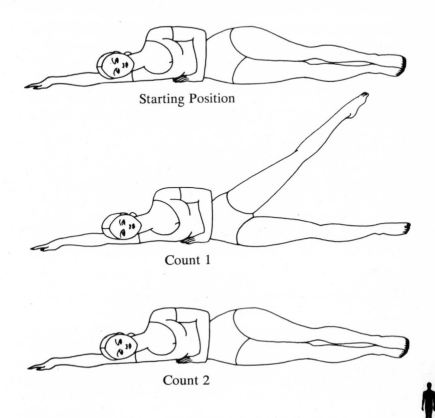

Starting Position

Count 1

Count 2

Side Leg Raise

Starting Position: Lie on left side with body in a straight line, left arm straight and extended under your head. Place palm of right hand on floor alongside your chest for support.

Action: Count 1. Lift right leg up as high as possible.
Count 2. Return to starting position.
After doing required number of repetitions on left side, turn and repeat on right side.

Cadence: Slow.

Repetitions: First week: 5 each side
Second week: 6 each side
Third week: 8 each side
Fourth week: 10 each side

Category: **Neck, Arms, Shoulders**

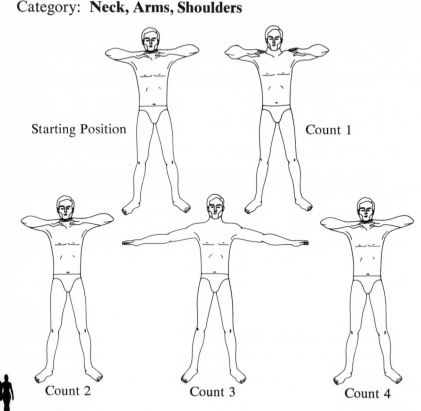

Starting Position

Count 1

Count 2

Count 3

Count 4

Arm Fling

Starting Position: Stand with feet separated shoulder width. Head up. Hold arms with elbows bent at shoulder level and fingers extended and touching in front of chest.

Action: Count 1. Fling elbows back as far as possible, keeping them at shoulder level.

Count 2. Return to starting position.

Count 3. Extend arms out straight and fling backward as far as possible, keeping them at shoulder level.

Count 4. Return to starting position.

Cadence: Fast pace.

Repetitions: First week: 5
Second week: 6
Third week: 8
Fourth week: 10

Category: **Cardiorespiratory System**

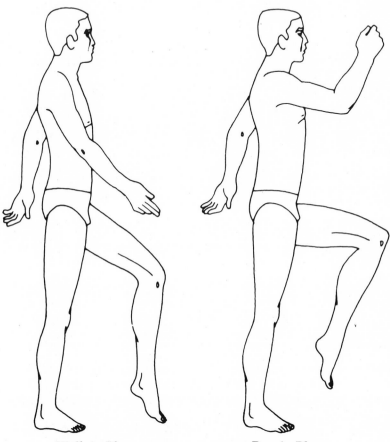

Walk-in-Place   *Run-in-Place*

Walk/Run-in-Place

Same as beginning level (page 161).

Repetitions: Walk/run in place or around the room for four to
six minutes, alternating 30 walking steps and 30
running steps.

MAINTENANCE LEVEL
Category: **Abdomen**

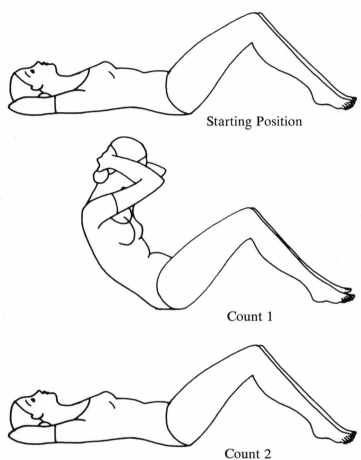

Starting Position

Count 1

Count 2

Bent-Knee Half-Curl

Same as beginning and intermediate levels, except hold
for six seconds.

Repetitions: First week: 8
Second week: 8
Third week: 9
Fourth week: 10

Category: **Trunk (Waist/Lower Back)**

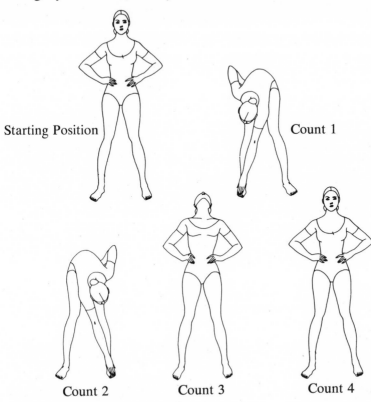

Starting Position

Count 1

Count 2

Count 3

Count 4

Alternate Toe-Touch Stretch

Starting Position: Stand with hands on hips, feet separated shoulder width.

Action: Count 1. With knees slightly bent, bend from waist and touch the left toe with the right hand.

Count 2. Twist and touch the right toe with the left hand.

Count 3. Return to standing position, bend backward, and stretch.

Count 4. Return to starting position.

Cadence: Moderate.

Repetitions: First week: 6
Second week: 8
Third week: 10
Fourth week: 12

Category: **Balance**

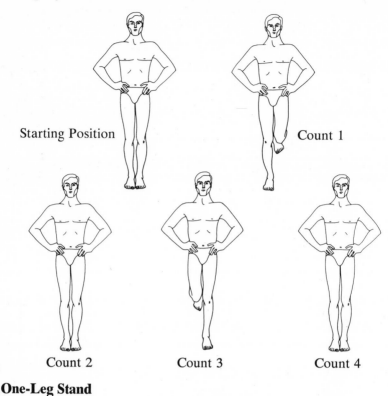

Starting Position   Count 1

Count 2   Count 3   Count 4

One-Leg Stand

Starting Position: Stand with feet together, hands on hips, head up, and looking straight ahead.

Action: Count 1. Lift your right foot off floor by bending your knee, balancing on your left foot for a count of five seconds.

               Count 2. Return to the standing position.

               Count 3. Repeat Count 1, but reverse the legs.

               Count 4. Return to the starting position.

Cadence: Slow.

Repetitions: First week: 5 each leg
Second week: 6 each leg
Third week: 7 each leg
Fourth week: 8 each leg

NOTE: Do some of the One-Leg Stands with your eyes open and some with your eyes closed.

Category: **Hips, Thighs, Buttocks**

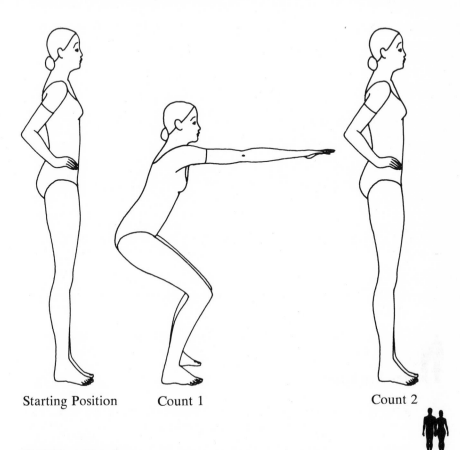

Starting Position   Count 1   Count 2

Half Knee Bend

Starting Position: Stand with hands on hips, feet separated about shoulder width.

Action: Count 1. Swing arms forward and up to shoulder height and bend knees about halfway, keeping your heels on the floor.

                 Count 2. Return to the starting position.

Cadence: Moderate.

Repetitions: First week: 6
                 Second week: 8
                 Third week: 10
                 Fourth week: 12

Category: **Neck, Arms, Shoulders**

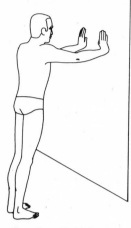

Starting Position

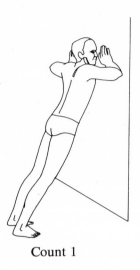

Count 1

Count 2

Wall Push-away

Starting Position: Stand at arm's length facing a wall. Place hands on wall shoulder width apart and at shoulder height. Feet should be separated about six inches.

Action: Count 1. Bend elbows, slowly lowering body toward the wall, turning head until your cheek touches the wall.

Count 2. Pushing with hands and straightening arms, return to the starting position.

Cadence: Moderate.

Repetitions: First week: 8
Second week: 10
Third week: 12
Fourth week: 14

NOTE: Practice Wall Push-away until you can keep heels on floor, with back and legs straight, throughout the exercise.

Category: **Cardiorespiratory System**

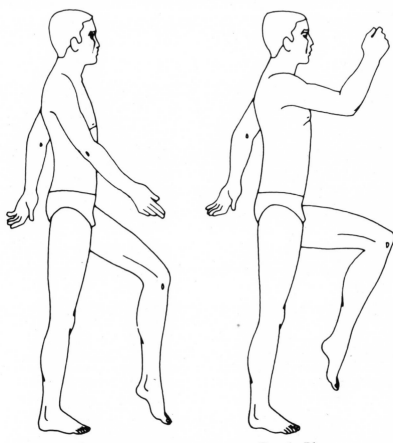

Walk-in-Place   *Run-in-Place*

Walk/Run-in-Place

Same as in beginning and intermediate levels.

Repetitions: Walk/run in place or around the room for six minutes, alternating 50 walking steps and 50 running
steps.

NOTE: See Chapter 3, The Walk/Run Plan, for outdoor cardiorespiratory conditioning by sex and age up to age 70.

SECTION III

Fitness Plus

CHAPTER 10

BBC–Beyond Basic Conditioning for All Ages

BBC is an optional program that serves a dual purpose, which is illustrated in two charts. The first chart, Guide to Sports Conditioning, tells you how to increase muscular strength and endurance for a particular sport. This guide is specific. For example, some exercises are designed to strengthen your grip for better control of a racquet, bat, golf club, or fishing rod. Other exercises are keyed to hit a ball harder, throw a longer pass, or swim stronger. You select the exercises that will help overcome a particular weakness in your favorite sport.

The other chart, Dumbbell Routines for Overall Conditioning, contains three different routines that either replace or supplement your basic muscular-conditioning program. For some of you the Basic Five or Six may be all that you require to maintain vigor and strength through a normal day of work and leisure. However, if you require an extra degree of fitness for sports, business, or your private life, then you may go on to BBC. These exercises are designed to develop your muscular strength and endurance beyond the maintenance level of basic conditioning; they are not for body building.

More Myth Shattering

The BBC exercises require the use of inexpensive dumbbells, but before going into detail let's dispel some myths that might scare you off.

One myth concerns the fear in women that dumbbells will develop bulky, ugly muscles. This notion has been disproved by studies in which women have used weights to increase muscular strength substantially. The largest increase in their biceps was less than a quarter of an inch, practically indiscernible. Of course, you can prove this out for yourself by checking your muscles daily in a mirror.

Another false notion, common to both men and women, is the fear that dumbbells will make them muscle-bound. Or, the reasoning goes this way: The stronger you become, the more likely you are to be muscle-bound. This is a matter we take seriously at West Point because to say you're muscle-bound is just another way of saying that you've lost flexibility.

We recently conducted an extensive study at West Point to determine the relationship between increasing strength and flexibility. We learned that properly designed exercises not only increase strength but also improve flexibility. Similarly, the exercises in the BBC are designed not only to increase muscular strength and endurance but also to improve your flexibility. Again, rest assured that there's no possibility of becoming muscle-bound when you use this BBC program.

How to Choose Your Equipment

The only equipment required for BBC are dumbbells, which range in weight from as little as 2 or 3 pounds up to 50 or more pounds each. Since the object of BBC is not to develop new, bulky muscles, you will not be working with extremely heavy weights.

In choosing dumbbells for yourself, follow the same rule the cadets use. Choose the weight that allows you to do the exercise correctly. Take this book with you to a sport store and try out several exercises with dumbbells. If the dumbbells feel unwieldy, then try a lighter weight.

Here's a guess at how a family of five might choose dumbbells if they were all in fairly good condition:

The father—two sets, 10- and 20-pound dumbbells

The mother and teen-age daughter—3-, 5-, and 10-pound dumbbells

A teen-age son—5-, 10-, and 20-pound dumbbells

A child between the ages of 10 and 12—3- and 5-pound dumbbells

Generally, you use heavier dumbbells when working the leg muscles, the lighter dumbbells when working arms. It's recom-

mended that children between the ages of 10 and 12 be super-
vised in using dumbbells to assure that they do the exercises
correctly and to prevent them from working with weights that
are too heavy. Children under 10 should be encouraged to develop muscles on jungle gyms and low bars and with other
vigorous physical activity but not with weights and dumbbells.

Questions Asked About BBC

Q. *If you err, is it better to err on the side of buying dumbbells that are too light or are too heavy?*

A. If the dumbbells are too heavy, you probably won't do
the exercises correctly, which defeats the purpose. If it turns out
that the dumbbells feel too light, you can compensate for this
by doing the exercises more slowly. This increases the stress by
forcing the muscle to support the weight for a longer period of
time through the full range of motion.

Q. *Can I move onto heavier dumbbells if I want to go into
body building?*

A. You can move onto heavier dumbbells if you want to
further increase your strength, but you must understand that
this program is not for the professional football player or anyone
who wants to add body weight by increasing muscle bulk. If
this is your objective, you need the kind of equipment and expertise that you find in a gymnasium where a weight-training
program is offered under professional guidance.

Q. *If you condition yourself lifting dumbbells or other weights
and then stop, will the muscle turn to fat?*

A. No. That's another myth. Your muscle won't turn to fat
when you stop exercising and neither does fat turn to muscle
when one begins exercising. Like apples and oranges, muscle
and fat are two different things.

Q. *How hard do you work in the BBC program?*

A. The number of repetitions for each exercise vary according to the level of a person's strength and the weight of the
dumbbells. You repeat the exercise until you reach "momentary
muscular fatigue," which means that for the moment you can no
longer do the exercise, and then you move on to the next exercise.

As a rule we have cadets use a weight with which they can
perform at least 8 but not more than 12 repetitions. In the begin-

ning you may tire long before you reach 12 repetitions. However, if you find that 12 repetitions are not enough to fatigue your muscles, then you have three options: You may (1) increase the weight of the dumbbells by two or three pounds but not more than five, (2) exercise at a slower speed, or (3) increase the number of repetitions.

Generally, when you increase repetitions—and you may go as high as 25 or 30—you will develop a little more strength, but most of the benefit will be in increased muscular endurance.

Q. *How often should I work out with dumbbells?*

A. For maximum progress you should work every day because this is a program of relatively light weights that will not totally exhaust your muscles. However, in order to escape boredom, the first recommendation would be five days a week, which gives you two days a week to break away from the monotony. Next best is three alternate days a week. Two days a week is minimum.

You can juggle the schedule to your own needs. You could work with dumbbells three days a week and on alternate days go back to the Basic Five or Six. If you use the full range of dumbbell exercises, you can discontinue the muscular exercises in the basic conditioning plan. However, the dumbbells are not a substitute for the Walk/Run Plan.

Q. *What is the maintenance level of dumbbell exercises?*

A. That is up to you. When you have developed a strength level that meets your needs, then you should continue to exercise at that level at least two, but preferably three, times a week in order to maintain it. Always remember that if you stop exercising, you will lose conditioning rapidly. If you stop using dumbbells, then return to the maintenance level of the Basic Five or Six to retain some of the strength and endurance you've worked for.

Q. *Suppose I merely want to select a few dumbbell exercises to improve my game?*

A. You can begin doing that at any time, no matter what your level of basic conditioning. The important thing is to select the proper weight based on your level of conditioning. You must continue with the full range of the Basic Five or Six to maintain comprehensive conditioning.

THREE DUMBBELL ROUTINES FOR
OVERALL CONDITIONING

These routines are for the person who wants to go beyond the basic conditioning program in building muscular strength and endurance.

If you have completed all three levels of the Basic Five or Six, you are ready to start with DB Routine 1. After you have been working with Routine 1 for four weeks, at least three days each week, you can switch to either of the other routines. Then you can switch back and forth between routines at will. However, once you start a routine, stay with it for at least three successive workouts. The exercises that make up the routines are described starting on page 185.

The purpose in having three equivalent exercise routines is to give you a choice of exchanging exercises to help ward off boredom. However, if you select exercises for sports or if you interchange routines, remember to exercise the muscle groups in the order that is shown on the following chart.

DUMBBELL ROUTINES FOR OVERALL CONDITIONING

	Routine 1		Routine 2		Routine 3	
	Exercise	Number	Exercise	Number	Exercise	Number
Warm-up	Body Swing	19 DB	Body swing	19 DB	Body swing	19 DB
Legs:						
Thighs	Half-squat	24 DB	Forward lunge	23 DB	Step-up	26 DB
Calves	Heel rise	25 DB	Heel rise	25 DB	Heel rise	25 DB
Torso:						
Chest	Bench press	15 DB	Straight-arm pull-over	16 DB	Supine horizontal arm lift	5 DB
Upper back[a]	Bent-over row	17 DB	Upright row	18 DB	Bent-over lateral raise	7 DB
Lower back	Good morning	22 DB	Good morning	22 DB	Good morning	22 DB
Shoulders	Arms-sideward lift	1 DB	Arms-forward lift	2 DB	Shoulder rotation	6 DB
Arms:						
Upper (front)	Biceps curl	8 DB	Biceps curl	8 DB	Biceps curl	8 DB
Upper (back)	Triceps press	9 DB	Sitting press	10 DB	Triceps press	9 DB
Lower	Wrist roller[b]	14 DB	Wrist roller[b]	14 DB	Wrist roller[b]	14 DB
Lower	Forearm twist	13 DB	Forearm twist	13 DB	Forearm twist	13 DB
Waist:						
Sides	Side bend	20 DB	Side bend	20 DB	Side bend	20 DB
Stomach	Bent-knee curl	21 DB	Bent-knee curl	21 DB	Bent-knee curl	21 DB

[a] Exercises 3 DB and 4 DB can be used as substitute exercises for the upper back.

[b] The Wrist Roller can be replaced with two exercises, 11 DB and 12 DB, either as a personal preference or if the stick and rope required for the Wrist Roller are not available.

GUIDE TO SPORTS CONDITIONING

Shoulders and Arms

Number	Exercise	Body Region	Sports and Activities
1 DB	Arms-sideward lift	Outer portions of shoulders	Tennis, golf, canoeing, archery, fencing, handball, swimming (breast, back, and crawl strokes), racquets, squash, baseball (throwing, batting), basketball
2 DB	Arms-forward lift	Front of shoulders and upper chest	Same as 1 DB
3 DB	Arms-backward lift	Back of shoulders and upper back	Swimming (all strokes), golf, baseball (batting), canoeing, tennis (backhand), racquets, squash, archery
4 DB	Prone horizontal arm lift	Back of shoulders and upper back	Same as 3 DB
5 DB	Supine horizontal arm lift	Front of shoulders and chest	Same as 1 DB
6 DB	Shoulder rotation	Front and back of shoulders	Same as 1 DB. Very good for throwing
7 DB	Bent-over lateral raise (can substitute for 3 DB)	Back of shoulders and upper back	Same as 3 DB
8 DB	Biceps curl	Front of upper arms	Swimming (back stroke), archery, wrestling, judo, lifting with arms
9 DB	Triceps press	Back of upper arms	Swimming (breast stroke), baseball (throwing and batting), boxing, karate, basketball, fencing, pole vaulting
10 DB	Sitting press	Back of upper arms, shoulders and upper back	Same as 1 DB and 9 DB
11 DB	Wrist extension	Forearms, wrists and hands	Tennis (backhand stroke), grip strength, fishing (casting)
12 DB	Wrist curl	Wrists	Tennis, baseball (throwing, batting), golf, handball, grip strength
13 DB	Forearm twist	Forearms, wrists and hands	Tennis, baseball (throwing, batting), boxing, fencing

(Continued on following page)

Number	Exercise	Body Region	Sports and Activities
14 DB	Wrist roller	Forearms, wrists and hands	Grip strength: any activity in which you hold equipment (same as 11 DB and 12 DB)
Torso, Waist, Abdomen, Lower Back, Arms			
15 DB	Bench press	Chest and back of upper arms	Tennis, swimming, baseball (throwing, batting), boxing, fencing, judo, karate, wrestling, football (passing)
16 DB	Straight-arm pull-over	Front and sides of chest	Swimming, baseball (throwing), golf, tennis, handball, boxing
17 DB	Bent-over row	Upper back, sides of chest, front of arms	Tennis, golf, swimming (all strokes), baseball (throwing, batting), handball, fencing, archery
18 DB	Upright row	Upper back, sides of chest, shoulders	Wrestling, football (passing), swimming, baseball (batting and throwing)
19 DB	Body Swing	Lower back and shoulders	Swimming (racing start), baseball (batting), handball, golf
20 DB	Side bend	Sides of trunk	All sports, posture, appearance, and general fitness
21 DB	Bent-knee curl	Abdomen	Same as for 20 DB
22 DB	Good morning	Lower back	Baseball (batting), golf, swimming, diving, tumbling
Legs and Hips			
23 DB	Forward lunge	Thighs and hips	Skiing, skating, jumping, kicking, swimming (kicks), bicycling
24 DB	Half-squat	Thighs and buttocks	Skiing, skating, football and soccer (kicking), swimming (kicks), quick starts in running
25 DB	Heel rise	Calf muscles	Quick starts in running, skating, jumping, skiing
26 DB	Step-up	Front of thighs and buttocks	Skiing, running, jumping, skating, football and soccer (kicking), bicycling

DUMBBELL EXERCISES

To determine which of these exercises you should do and the proper sequence, see preceding charts. All exercises must be performed correctly for maximum development and flexibility. Repetitions are performed until you reach "momentary muscular fatigue," which means until your muscles are too tired to repeat the exercise. Then you go on to the next exercise as designated by the chart. Unless otherwise specified, perform exercises at a moderate cadence.

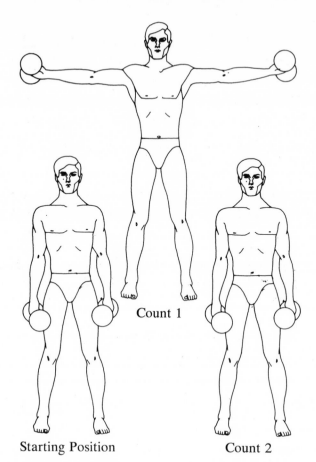

Count 1

Starting Position   Count 2

1 DB—Arms-Sideward Lift

Purpose: To develop outer portions of shoulders.

Starting Position: Stand erect with feet about shoulder width apart, palms facing the body, and dumbbells at sides.

Action: Count 1. Lift the dumbbells directly sideways to the horizontal level.
Count 2. Lower to starting position.
Repeat.

Alternative: Exercise may be performed by lifting dumbbells to overhead position on Count 2.

Instructions: Throughout exercise maintain proper body alignment while lifting and lowering dumbbells.

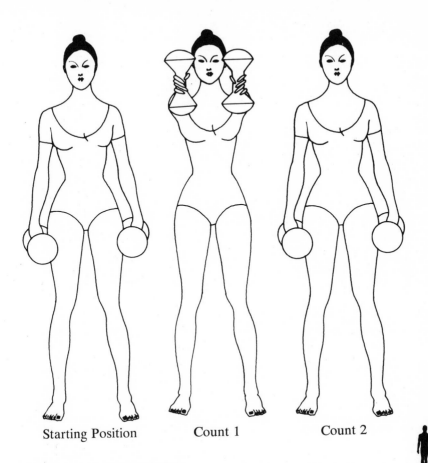

Starting Position   Count 1   Count 2

2 DB—Arms-Forward Lift

Purpose: To develop front of shoulders and upper chest.

Starting Position: Stand erect with feet about shoulder width apart, palms facing the body, and dumbbells at sides.

Action: Count 1. Lift the dumbbells forward to the horizontal position.
Count 2. Lower slowly to the starting position.
Repeat.

Alternative: Exercise may be performed by lifting dumbbells completely overhead.

Instructions: Throughout exercise keep your head erect and body in good alignment.

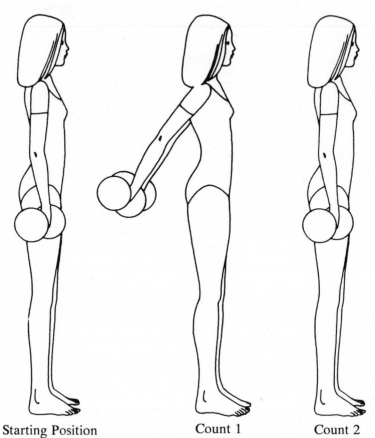

Starting Position   Count 1   Count 2

3 DB—Arms-Backward Lift

Purpose: To develop back of shoulders and upper back.

Starting Position: Stand with feet separated shoulder width, palms facing the rear, and dumbbells at sides.

Action: Count 1. Raise the dumbbells backward and upward as far as possible without bending the trunk or hips.

Count 2. Lower dumbbells slowly to starting position.

Repeat.

Instructions: Keep head erect and body in good alignment throughout movement.

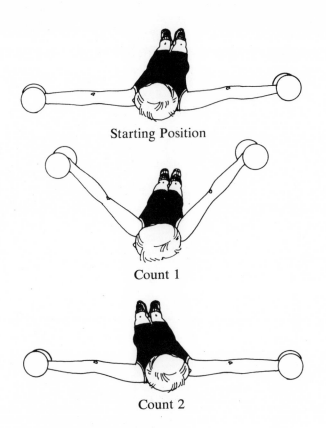

Starting Position

Count 1

Count 2

4 DB—Prone Horizontal Arm Lift

Purpose: To develop back of shoulders and back.

Starting Position: Lie in prone position with arms extended out from shoulders at horizontal level. Dumbbells are grasped with the palms facing the floor. (Body may rest in prone position on exercise board or table with arms extended outward at horizontal level or somewhat toward floor.)

Action: Count 1. Raise arms directly upward toward the ceiling as far as possible.
Count 2. Lower slowly to the starting position.
Repeat.

Instructions: Make certain to keep your legs and feet on floor or bench throughout the movement. The head should be held steady, face downward.

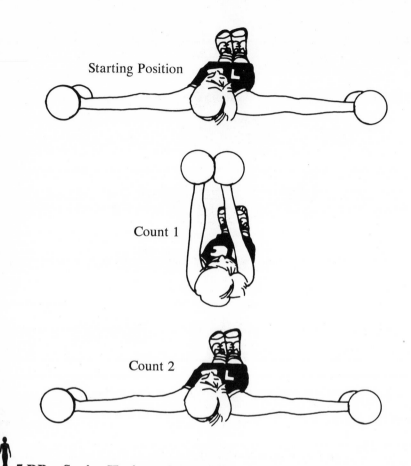

Starting Position

Count 1

Count 2

5 DB—Supine Horizontal Arm Lift

Purpose: To develop front of shoulders and chest.

Starting Position: Lie in supine position with arms extended out from the shoulders at horizontal level. Dumbbells are grasped with the palms facing upward. (Body may rest on inclined exercise board or table with arms out at your sides at maximum-stretch position.)

Action: Count 1. Raise arms directly upward to perpendicular position above shoulders.
Count 2. Lower slowly to the starting position. Repeat.

Instructions: The head should be kept in a steady position with your face directed upward.

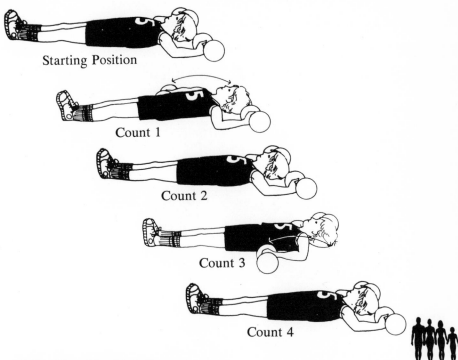

Starting Position

Count 1

Count 2

Count 3

Count 4

6 DB—Shoulder Rotation

Purpose: To develop front and back of shoulders.

Starting Position: Lying supine with upper arms directed out from shoulders; elbows bent at right angles causing the forearms to lie along the floor, parallel to body; hands at level with top of head, palms directed upwards. Knees may be extended, or may be bent with feet flat on the floor.

Action: Count 1. Lift dumbbell in right hand and rotate the weight until it is resting on the floor by waist. Keep upper arm and elbow in contact with the floor.

Count 2. Rotate right arm back to the starting position.

Count 3. Repeat Count 1, using left arm.

Count 4. Rotate back to starting position.

Instructions: The movement should be uninterrupted. Greater range of movement can be obtained by performing the exercise from a bench position.

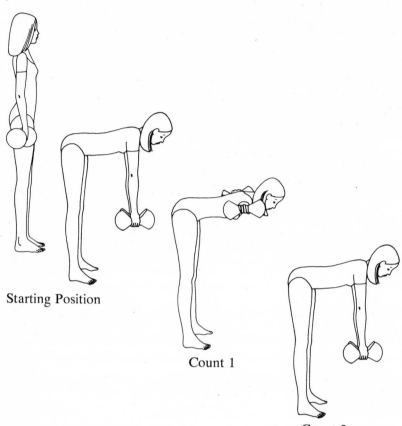

Starting Position

Count 1

Count 2

7 DB—Bent-over Lateral Raise

Purpose:　To develop back of shoulders and upper back.

Starting Position:　Stand with feet separated shoulder width. Hold a dumbbell at each side with palms facing each other. Bend forward at the hips, allowing the arms to hang straight down from the shoulders.

Action:　Count 1.　Keeping arms straight, slowly raise the dumbbells in an arc until the arms are straight out from the body.
　　　　　Count 2.　Slowly lower in the same arc to the starting position.
　　　　　Repeat.

Instructions:　Keep the upper body parallel with the floor throughout the exercise.

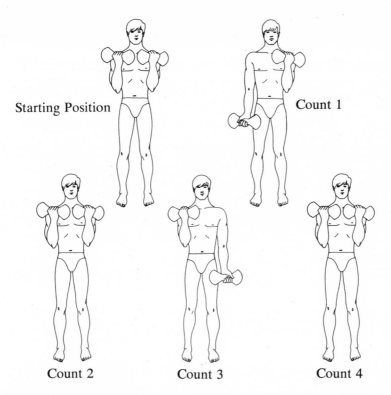

Starting Position

Count 1

Count 2

Count 3

Count 4

8 DB—Biceps Curl

Purpose: To develop front of upper arms.

Starting Position: Stand with feet separated less than shoulder width with a dumbbell in each hand and arms bent so that the dumbbells are about at shoulder height and the palms facing the shoulders.

Action: Count 1. Lower right arm slowly until dumbbell is beside right thigh and the arm is straight.
Count 2. Raise your right arm slowly until dumbbell is returned to the starting position.
Count 3. Repeat Count 1 using left arm.
Count 4. Return left arm to the starting position.
Repeat from Count 1.

Instructions: Keep trunk erect at all times. Do not bend backward in order to lift the weight. Do the exercise slowly and use only the arm muscles as you lift the dumbbells. Keep elbows at sides throughout the movement.

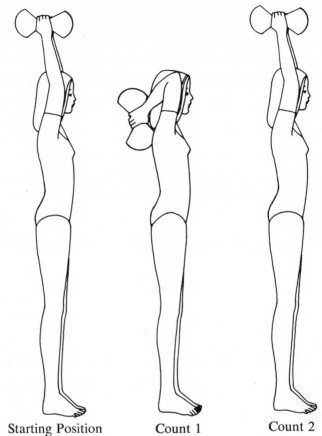

Starting Position   Count 1   Count 2

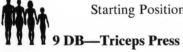

9 DB—Triceps Press

Purpose: To develop back of upper arms.

Starting Position: Standing erect, feet separated shoulder width, hold the dumbbells overhead in a full arm-press position. The palms of your hands should face each other.

Action: Count 1. Lower the dumbbells slowly behind your neck.

Count 2. Raise the dumbbells back up overhead. Repeat.

Instructions: When dumbbells are at lowest position, elbows should be pointed upward. Keep your body stabilized and place all responsibility for movement on your triceps (muscles on back of upper arm).

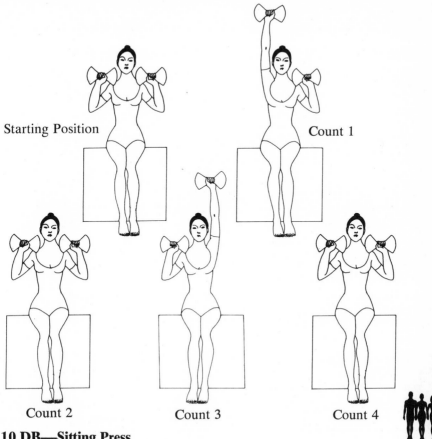

Starting Position

Count 1

Count 2

Count 3

Count 4

10 DB—Sitting Press

Purpose: To develop upper back, shoulders, and back of upper arms.

Starting Position: Sit on a chair or a stool. Keeping your back straight, hold a dumbbell in each hand at shoulder height with palms facing forward.

Action: Count 1. Push right hand over head until your arm is fully extended. Keep palm facing forward.

Count 2. Lower right hand to starting position.

Count 3. Repeat Count 1 using left hand.

Count 4. Return to starting position.

Repeat.

Instructions: Although this exercise can be done while standing, there is less strain on back if you are seated.

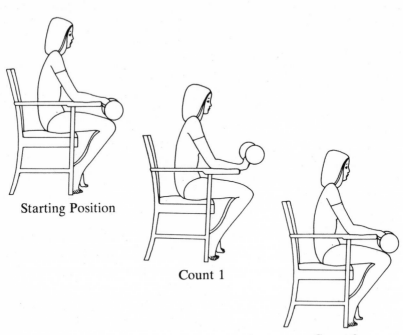

Starting Position

Count 1

Count 2

11 DB—Wrist Extension

Purpose: To develop forearms, wrists, and hands.

Starting Position: Sit on stool or chair with forearm resting on the table but wrist and hand completely off the table. Grasp dumbbell with palm facing downward and permit the dumbbell to take the wrist to a maximum flexed position.

Action: Count 1. Lift the dumbbell by extending the wrist upward through its maximum range of movement.

Count 2. Lower the dumbbell slowly back to the starting position.

Repeat.

Repeat exercise with other forearm.

Instructions: Your wrist must be freely movable at the table so that the maximum range of motion is available. Your entire forearm must remain on the table throughout the movement.

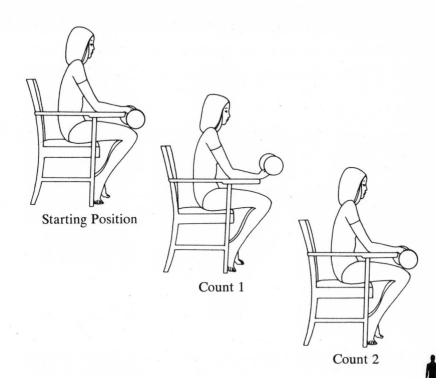

Starting Position

Count 1

Count 2

12 DB—Wrist Curl

Purpose: To develop forearms, wrists, and hands.

Starting Position: Sit on stool or chair with your forearm resting on the table but your wrist and hand completely off the table. Grasp the dumbbell with the palm upward. Allow the dumbbell to take the wrist into a full-stretch position.

Action: Count 1. Lift the dumbbell through the maximum range of movement.

Count 2. Lower the dumbbell slowly back to the starting position.

Repeat.

Repeat exercise with other hand.

Instructions: Your entire forearm must remain on the table throughout the movement. Your wrist and hand must be completely off the table to permit full range of movement.

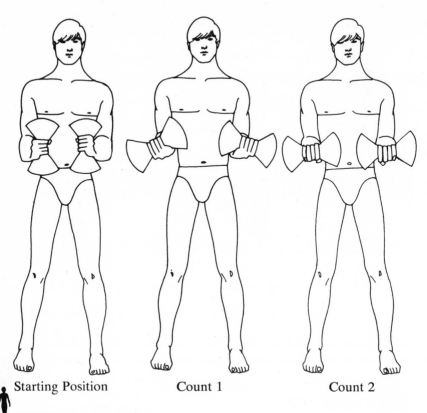

Starting Position   Count 1   Count 2

13 DB—Forearm Twist

Purpose: To develop forearms, wrists, and hands.

Starting Position: Stand with feet separated shoulder width. Elbows against side and bent forward at a 90-degree angle. Hold a dumbbell in each hand with palms facing each other.

Action: Count 1. Rotate both hands to the palm-up position and continue to rotate in the same direction as far as you can.

Count 2. Reverse the direction of rotation toward the palm-down position and continue to turn as far as you can.

Alternately repeat counts 1 and 2.

Instructions: This may also be done in the sitting position, using the same chair and table as for exercises 11 DB and 12 DB.

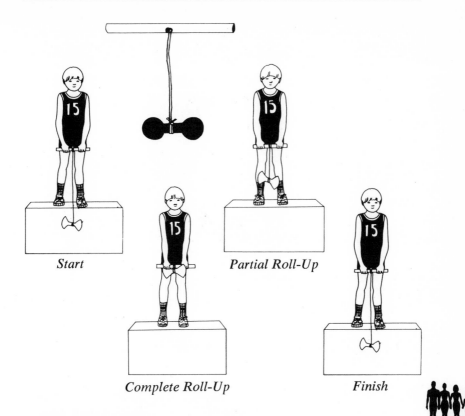

Start   **Partial Roll-Up**

Complete Roll-Up   **Finish**

14 DB—Wrist Roller

Purpose: To develop forearms, wrists, and hands.

Starting Position: (Prepare the wrist roller by getting a round stick about 15 to 18 inches long and about the thickness of a large broomstick. Attach a clothesline rope 4 to 5 feet long to the stick with a nail or by drilling hole through stick. Tie other end of rope to dumbbell.) Stand with feet separated shoulder width. Arms at sides with palms down holding the handle of the wrist roller.

Action: Count 1. Wind rope up on handle.
Count 2. Slowly unwind rope.
Count 3. Repeat Count 1 with palms facing up.
Count 4. Repeat Count 2 with palms facing up.
Repeat from Count 1.

Instructions: A longer rope can be used for this exercise if you are standing on a bench or sturdy chair.

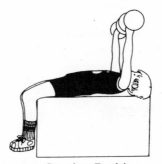

Starting Position

Count 1

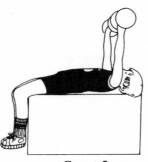

Count 2

15 DB—Bench Press

Purpose: To develop chest muscles and back of upper arms.

Starting Position: Lie on back on a sturdy bench with arms straight out. Hold a dumbbell in each hand with palms facing away from body.

Action: Count 1. Lower the dumbbells to the chest and pause.

Count 2. Push the dumbbells back to starting position.

Repeat.

Instructions: Keep your back flat on the bench.

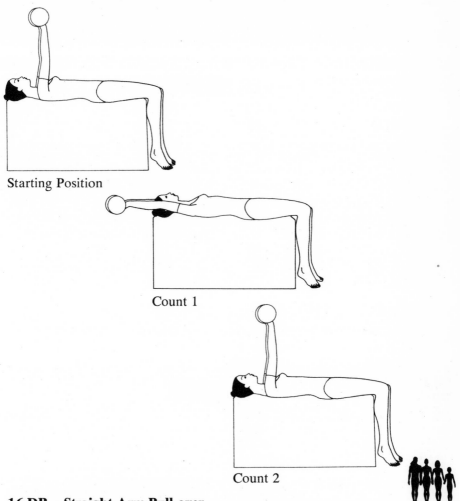

Starting Position

Count 1

Count 2

16 DB—Straight-Arm Pull-over

Purpose: To develop front and sides of chest.

Starting Position: Lie on back on the floor or on a sturdy bench with arms straight up. Hold a dumbbell in each hand with palms facing up.

Action: Count 1. Keeping your arms straight, lower both dumbbells in an arc to a position directly above your head and pause.
Count 2. Return dumbbells to starting position.
Repeat.

Instructions: Keep your back flat on floor or bench.

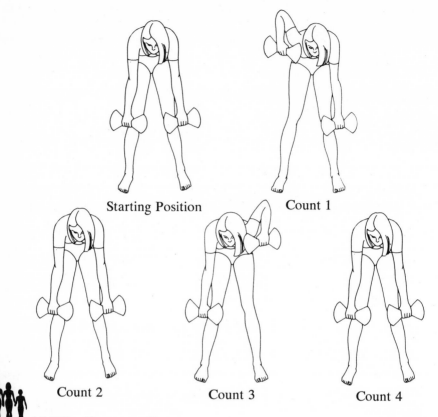

Starting Position   Count 1

Count 2   Count 3   Count 4

17 DB—Bent-over Row

Purpose: To develop upper back, sides of chest, and front of upper arms.

Starting Position: Stand with feet shoulder width apart, knees slightly bent. Bend forward at the waist until your trunk is parallel with the floor. Hold the dumbbells at arm's length directly below the shoulders.

Action: Count 1. Raise your right hand, bringing the dumbbell to the right shoulder.
Count 2. Lower right hand to starting position.
Count 3. Raise your left hand, bringing dumbbell to left shoulder.
Count 4. Lower left hand to starting position.
Repeat from Count 1.

Instructions: Keep your knees bent slightly to take the pressure off your back.

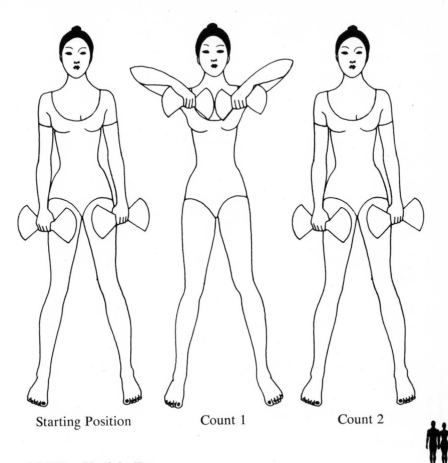

Starting Position   Count 1   Count 2

18 DB—Upright Row

Purpose: To develop shoulders, upper back, and sides of chest.

Starting Position: Stand with feet shoulder width apart. Hold dumbbells at arm's length in front of your thighs, with palms facing to the rear.

Action: Count 1. Raise the dumbbells to the chin, keeping your elbows above the level of your hands at all times.

          Count 2. Return to starting position.

          Repeat.

Instructions: Keep your palms facing the rear at all times. Your hands should be less than shoulder width apart.

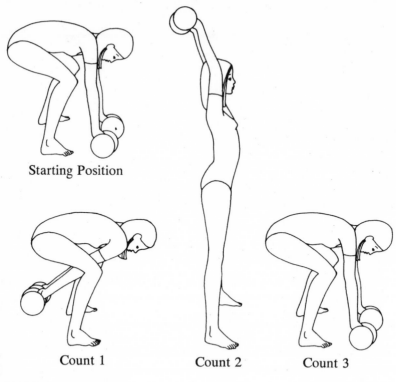

Starting Position

Count 1   Count 2   Count 3

19 DB—Body Swing

Purpose: To develop lower back and shoulders.

Starting Position: Place dumbbells on floor in front of you. With feet more than shoulder width apart, bend from the knees, and pick up the dumbbells. Keep your elbows and wrists locked in straight line.

Action: Count 1. Swing the dumbbells back between your legs.

Count 2. Swing dumbbells in an arc forward and up over head, continuing to keep elbows and wrists locked.

Count 3. Swing dumbbells in an arc back to Count 1.

Repeat from Count 1.

Instructions: When swinging dumbbells, keep your knees slightly bent until your arms are overhead. This is a continuous rhythmic exercise to be performed at a moderate cadence.

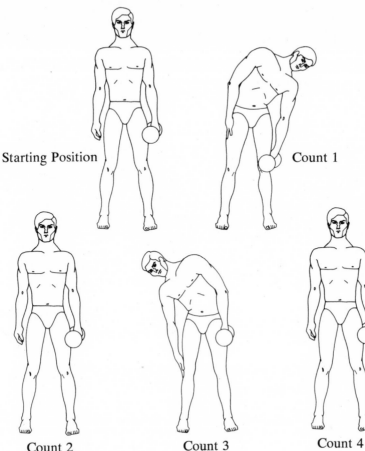

Starting Position

Count 1

Count 2

Count 3

Count 4

20 DB—Side Bend

Purpose: To develop muscles at the sides of the trunk.

Starting Position: Stand with feet shoulder width apart, holding a dumbbell in the left hand at arm's length alongside the thigh.

Action: Count 1. Bend to the left, lowering the dumbbell below your left knee.

Count 2. Return to the starting position.

Count 3. Bend to the right, touching your right hand below the right knee.

Count 4. Return to the starting position.

Change the dumbbell to the right hand and repeat the exercise.

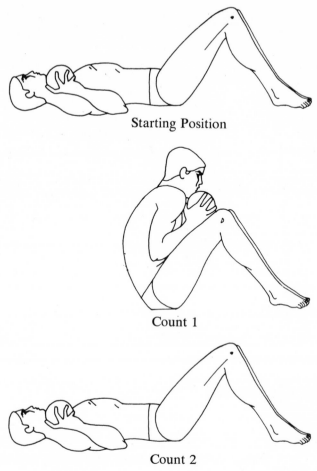

Starting Position

Count 1

Count 2

21 DB—Bent-Knee Curl

Purpose: To develop abdominal muscles.

Starting Position: Lie on back with knees bent in an angle of 45 to 90 degrees. Feet on floor. Hold dumbbells high against chest while doing exercise.

Action: Count 1. Tucking chin into chest, curl as far forward as possible into a sitting position.
Count 2. Return to starting position.
Repeat.

Instructions: Increase level of stress by resting feet on chair.

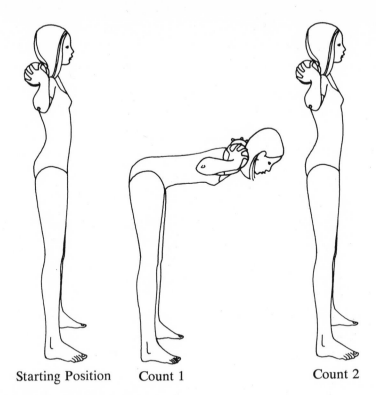

Starting Position   Count 1   Count 2

22 DB—Good Morning

Purpose: To develop lower back.

Starting Position: Stand with feet separated shoulder width and knees locked. With both hands hold one dumbbell behind your neck.

Action: Count 1. Bend forward at the waist until your upper body is below parallel with the floor. Hold for count of two seconds.

Count 2. Return to starting position.

Repeat.

Instructions: Keep head up at all times. Keep your hips forward over your ankles; do not thrust hips back. You should have the feeling that you are forward on your toes rather than back on your heels when you are in the bent-over position.

CAUTION: If you suffer from lower-back pain, do not do this exercise until you consult with your physician.

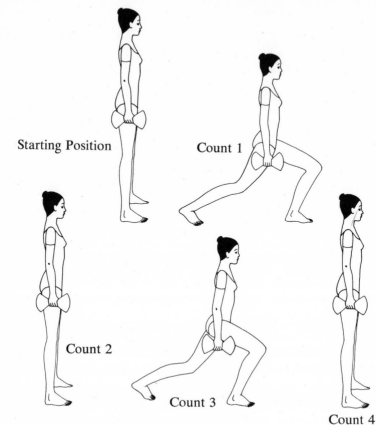

Starting Position

Count 1

Count 2

Count 3

Count 4

23 DB—Forward Lunge

Purpose: To develop thighs and hips.

Starting Position: Stand with feet less than shoulder width apart, holding dumbbells at arm's length at the sides.

Action: Count 1. Take big step forward with left foot while keeping right foot in place, bending both knees.

Count 2. Return to starting position.

Count 3. Take big step forward with right foot while keeping left foot in place, bending both knees.

Count 4. Return to starting position.

Repeat from Count 1.

Instructions: Keep your trunk upright and back straight throughout exercise.

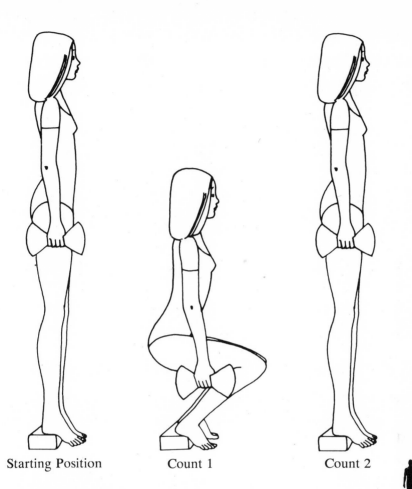

Starting Position   Count 1   Count 2

24 DB—Half-Squat

Purpose: To develop thighs and buttocks.

Starting Position: Stand with feet shoulder width apart, holding
                 dumbbells at arm's length at the sides.

Action: Count 1. Bend your knees until your thighs are
                 parallel to the floor. Keep your back
                 straight.
                 Count 2. Return to the starting position.
                 Repeat.

Instructions: Placing a thick book under your heels will help you
                 maintain balance.

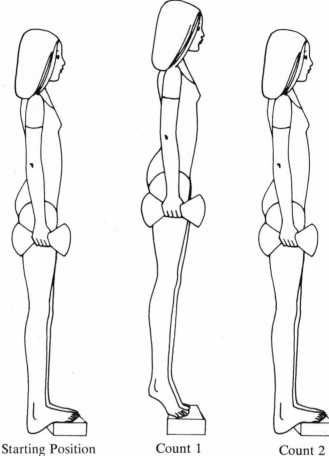

Starting Position   Count 1   Count 2

25 DB—Heel Rise

Purpose: To develop calf muscles.

Starting Position: Stand with toes elevated on a thick book or on a two- to three-inch-thick board. Hold dumbbells alongside body.

Action: Count 1. Raise heels off floor.
                 Count 2. Slowly return to starting position with heels resting on floor.
                 Repeat.

Instructions: Raise your heels as high as possible.

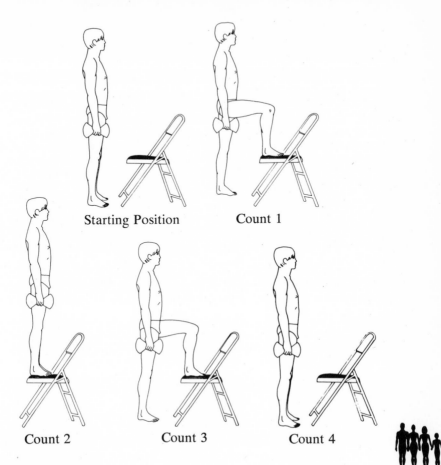

Starting Position   Count 1

Count 2   Count 3   Count 4

26 DB—Step-up

Purpose: To develop front of thighs and buttocks.

Starting Position: Stand in front of a sturdy chair or at the bottom of a stairway. Hold a dumbbell in each hand.

Action: Count 1. Place your left foot on the chair (or on the second step of the stairs).

Count 2. Straighten left leg and bring your right foot up alongside your left foot.

Count 3. With your left foot step down from the chair or step.

Count 4. Return your right foot to the floor.

Repeat.

Instructions: Change the starting foot every two repetitions so that each leg gets the same amount of work.

CHAPTER 11

Posture:
How to Look Good

Every year they come to West Point, a thousand or more plebes, and their posture ranges from not very good to very bad. On the day they arrive, we begin taking side-view and back-view photographs of each and every man and woman to analyze the position of the head, shoulders, chest, abdomen, back, pelvis, and knees. Good posture has been a major concern at West Point for over 170 years, and West Point probably knows and does more about improving posture than any other institution.

Many of the postural problems we see can be corrected with a simple procedure, and we'll tell you about it, but we'll also give you corrective exercises for body deviations that are more severe. But since we've learned at West Point that up to 90 percent of the new cadets know nothing about posture except that their parents nagged at them to "stand straight," perhaps we ought to assume that there's a general misunderstanding about both good posture and military bearing.

What Is Good Posture?

Many people think of military bearing as being the ramrod look with chest stuck way out, shoulders forced back, and chin tucked in so tight that the back of your neck aches. Not so, because this is unhealthy and a strain on muscles and joints. At West Point military bearing is based on what physiologists and biomechanists know to be a healthy body stance. You'll discover that military bearing and good posture are virtually identical.

In both good posture and the military position of attention, the body alignment is exactly the same. The body weight centers

212

over the ankle bone with a vertical line cutting through the middle of the knee, hip, center of the shoulder tip, and finally the ear lobe. The only difference between the military and civilian stance is that the position of attention calls for straight elbows with thumbs touching the middle of the thigh and heels together with the feet at a 45-degree angle.

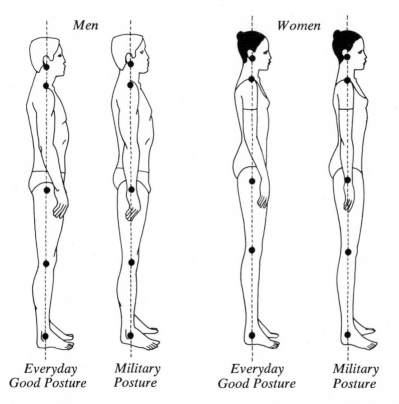

Men		*Women*	
Everyday Good Posture	*Military Posture*	*Everyday Good Posture*	*Military Posture*

The difference between everyday good posture and the military posture of attention is slight but distinctive. At attention the figure is a little more chesty; the elbows are straight with the thumb positioned along the middle of the thigh, and the heels are together with feet pointing outward at a 45-degree angle. Note that this is not the exaggerated "movie version" of attention, which is tensed, knotted, and so cramped that it actually damages proper body alignment.

The heavy numbered dots refer to the five checkpoints of good body alignment. A plumb line dropped from an overhead position alongside the body would fall through the lobe of the ear, the tip of the shoulder, the middle of the hips, slightly in back of the knee cap, and slightly in front of the ankle bone.

Neither perfect posture nor the position of attention is recommended as a constant. If you stop to talk to a friend, you're not going to be at attention. If you're at a party holding a glass in one hand, your feet are going to be separated, you'll likely be shifting weight from one hip to the other, and your head will probably drop down to listen to the talk. However, one of the subtle effects of learning good posture is that it carries over into your appearance even when you relax in social situations.

At West Point we play host to many visitors, ranging from presidents and princes to tourists and sightseers. We have learned that almost all of our visitors will comment on how good the cadets look. The visitors see cadets when they aren't at attention —when the cadets are walking between classes, stopping to talk to friends, in uniform or dressed informally for an athletic activity. Even with military bearing put aside, the cadets look good. The reason is that achieving correct posture requires good muscular balance. This in turn improves your coordination, and it all ends up bettering your appearance no matter what you are doing.

We insist on cadets learning good posture, but once learned they are encouraged to relax at the appropriate times. We also tell them that once in a while you can really slouch in a chair and let it all hang loose. That's bad posture, but it's harmful only if you slouch most of the time.

But Why a Major Project?

Why does West Point put so much emphasis on posture?

Some of it is based on military tradition, and some is practical psychology. Cadets become leaders, and their bearing must in itself inspire confidence, a factor that also applies to civilian careers. However, standing tall is not just a cliché. Good posture actually adds an inch or so to your height.

And then there's the aesthetics of good posture. Cadets and officers are expected to take pride in their appearance, and in this context also posture is important to civilians. If you are dieting and toning your muscles for appearance, then for the same reason you will want to improve your posture.

Another reason for emphasizing good posture has to do with fitness and health. Posture has a direct bearing on our comfort, work efficiency, and the internal function of our body. With good posture everything works better. On the other hand, poor posture may reduce blood circulation, induce shallower breathing, and bring on fatigue, backaches, and foot pain.

Another good reason for emphasizing posture becomes apparent as we grow older. All of us unconsciously go through every day resisting the pull of gravity in order to maintain an upright position. We have all seen older people who are losing the battle with gravity. It's the antigravity muscle groups that hold us erect. They are located in the calves, front of the thighs, buttocks, back (along the spine), and the abdomen. By learning and then maintaining good posture we help keep these muscle groups in condition to fight gravity and thus keep us erect into our later years.

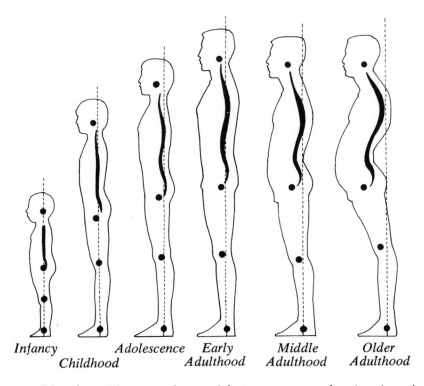

Infancy   *Adolescence* *Early*   *Middle*   *Older*
        Childhood   *Adulthood*   *Adulthood*   *Adulthood*

The above illustrates the usual but unnecessary deterioration of posture in a normal lifetime. Curves in neck, middle back, and lower back increase because of gravity, lack of vigor, ignorance, carelessness, and/or lack of pride.

Who's Throwing Those Bad Curves?

We are so accustomed to seeing people slump, tilt, and slouch that postural problems seem to be natural. They aren't. Although there are gentle spinal curves in the infant, some of these natural curves become stretched, twisted, and overstressed, and then one bad curve leads to another.

If a person has that "hang-dog" head look, which is an excessive curve in the neck area, it is usually at least the beginning of a dowager's hump because the upper back curves out to compensate for the stress in the neck. Another common problem is the abnormal forward curve, or sway, in the lower back that is accompanied by a tilting of the pelvis and a sagging abdomen. These postural problems are not only common to civilians but to most new cadets as well.

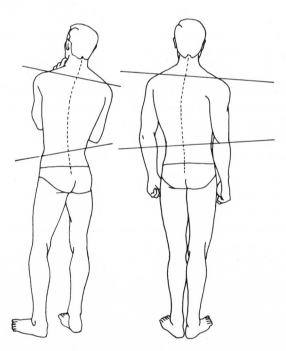

The above illustrations are based on actual photographs. On the left is the very common habit of resting on one leg. This eventually weakens muscles that normally would control body alignment. Finally, you have the result at the right: a person who actually thinks his body alignment is under control when, in fact, he can no longer assume proper posture.

There are many different explanations for poor posture. It can be brought on by an event like childbirth, or it can be caused by wearing high-heeled shoes or sitting in the wrong kind of chair. It can be caused by an occupational habit—the mailman carrying his bag over the same shoulder or, similarly, youngsters who carry their books on the same side over a dozen years of school. Generally, poor posture is a result of bad or lazy habits and ignorance.

One typical lazy habit is our conversational stance. Many of us, whether we stand with hands on hips or arms folded, get into the habit of resting our weight on one leg. If, for example, it's the right leg, then we tilt the pelvic area, which brings the right hip up, and the right shoulder down. Many of us repeat this lazy stance so frequently over the years that it permanently affects our body alignment.

HOW TO CORRECT POSTURAL PROBLEMS

In correcting poor posture we begin by identifying the problems with the Posture Score Sheet on page 218. You can score yourself by setting up three-way mirrors to get side and back views, but the better way is to work with a friend or someone in the family. If you are already concerned about your children's posture, work with them. Let your children diagnose your problems and you diagnose theirs.

If you find either yourself or your child scoring in the Poor column, or if you're uncertain how to classify your problems, we would prefer that you see a physician. Severe problems may have to do with bone structure, requiring the attention of an orthopedist. However, the majority of postural deviations are not extreme, and it's more likely that you will be able to do it yourself.

If you are already doing the Basic Five and Flexibility exercises, then your muscles are being prepared for posture improvement. All you may have to do is memorize and practice the five checkpoints noted in the illustration on page 215. This is the way you go about using the method:

Start from a standing position with your feet together and begin by working up from your feet.

POSTURE SCORE SHEET	Name _____			SCORING DATES				
	GOOD - 10	FAIR - 5	POOR - 0					
A HEAD — LEFT RIGHT	HEAD ERECT GRAVITY LINE PASSES DIRECTLY THROUGH CENTER	HEAD TWISTED OR TURNED TO ONE SIDE SLIGHTLY	HEAD TWISTED OR TURNED TO ONE SIDE MARKEDLY					
B SHOULDERS — LEFT RIGHT	SHOULDERS LEVEL (HORIZONTALLY)	ONE SHOULDER SLIGHTLY HIGHER THAN OTHER	ONE SHOULDER MARKEDLY HIGHER THAN OTHER					
B SPINE — LEFT RIGHT	SPINE STRAIGHT	SPINE SLIGHTLY CURVED LATERALLY	SPINE MARKEDLY CURVED LATERALLY					
B HIPS — LEFT RIGHT	HIPS LEVEL (HORIZONTALLY)	ONE HIP SLIGHTLY HIGHER	ONE HIP MARKEDLY HIGHER					
C ANKLES	FEET POINTED STRAIGHT AHEAD	FEET POINTED OUT	FEET POINTED OUT MARKEDLY ANKLES SAG IN (PRONATION)					
D NECK	NECK ERECT, CHIN IN, HEAD IN BALANCE DIRECTLY ABOVE SHOULDERS	NECK SLIGHTLY FORWARD, CHIN SLIGHTLY OUT	NECK MARKEDLY FORWARD, CHIN MARKEDLY OUT					
E UPPER BACK	UPPER BACK NORMALLY ROUNDED	UPPER BACK SLIGHTLY MORE ROUNDED	UPPER BACK MARKEDLY ROUNDED					
F TRUNK	TRUNK ERECT	TRUNK INCLINED TO REAR SLIGHTLY	TRUNK INCLINED TO REAR MARKEDLY					
F ABDOMEN	ABDOMEN FLAT	ABDOMEN PROTRUDING	ABDOMEN PROTRUDING AND SAGGING					
F LOWER BACK	LOWER BACK NORMALLY CURVED	LOWER BACK SLIGHTLY HOLLOW	LOWER BACK MARKEDLY HOLLOW					
ALL REPRODUCTION RIGHTS RESERVED © REEDCO INCORPORATED 8 EASTERLY AVENUE AUBURN N Y 13021 COPYRIGHT 1974			**TOTAL SCORES**					

("By permission of Reedco, Inc. Note that the authors have keyed these posture problems to corrective exercises which begin on page 220.)

Checkpoint 1—Ankles. Rock forward and backward until you get the feeling of how your body weight affects the different parts of your feet. Finally, place the weight in the area of your feet just forward of the ankle bone and hold it there.

Checkpoint 2—Knees. Keep your knees straight but not locked. Continue to balance your body weight between the heels and balls of your feet.

Checkpoint 3—Hips. Bring your hips back over your ankles. Buttocks, or tailbone, should be drawn downward to reduce forward tilt of the pelvis. Tighten your abdominal muscles because this helps to remove the sway in the lower back while flattening the stomach. Continue to keep your knees straight but without any stiffness. If you are wearing a belt, it should be horizontal and parallel with the ground all the way around.

Checkpoint 4—Shoulders. Your shoulders should be rolled back but relaxed. By relaxed, we mean that you should make no effort to squeeze your shoulder blades together, nor should you force your shoulders back. In this position your chest will raise moderately, and you should pull in your stomach.

Checkpoint 5—Head. The posture line, as you see in the illustration, passes through the ear lobe. This requires lifting and pulling your head back while keeping your chin level. Get the feeling of having a hook attached to the top of your head that, in turn, is attached to a piece of rope that runs through a pulley attached to the ceiling. Pretend that someone is pulling on the rope and is trying to lift you off the ground. That is the feeling we want the cadets to have when we say, "Stand tall."

In the beginning it helps to have someone make sure you are following through on the five checkpoints, and then it becomes do-it-yourself therapy. Most cadets can assume good posture when they understand and practice the five checkpoints but about 10 to 20 percent of the new cadets have long-standing and sometimes extreme postural deviations caused by muscular imbalance.

Following are some of the exercises that can be used at home for all but the most severe postural problems. (If you're not certain how to classify your own problems, consult with a physician and take along this book.) Correcting extreme postural deviations takes time: about three to four weeks of daily exercise before you see a change taking place.

THE POSTURE EXERCISES

These postural exercises have been selected because they require no special equipment and can be performed at home. Each of the exercises is keyed by letter to the posture deviations illustrated in the Posture Score Sheet.

A. Posture Deviation: Head Tilt, Either Left or Right

Exercise: **Side Neck Bend**

Purpose: To correct the head tilt by stretching the muscles on the side of the neck to which the head is tilted and strengthening the muscles on the opposite side.

Action: If your head is tilted to the left, begin by attempting to touch the right ear to the right shoulder. When your neck is bent as far as it will go, hold for a count of ten. If your head is tilted to the right, reverse the procedure.

Progression: Begin with three repetitions. Increase by one repetition each week until the deviation is corrected. You should try to perform this exercise two or three times daily. Once the deviation is corrected, perform the exercise to both sides in order to keep muscle tension balanced.

B. Posture Deviation: A C Curve in the Spine, Causing Uneven Shoulders and Hips

Exercises: **1. Unilateral Side Bend**
2. Vertical Hang

Purpose: To stretch the muscles on the concave side of the C curve and strengthen the muscles on the convex side. In addition, vertical hang uses your body weight to help to straighten the spine.

Action: 1. Raise your arm on the concave side of the C curve to a straight overhead position. Do an ordinary side bend but only in the direction of the convex side for postural correction (see page 34 for description and illustration of side bends). Bend as far as possible and hold for a count of ten. Repeat side bend five times.

2. Hang by both hands from a horizontal bar for one minute. Relax and follow with two repetitions.

Progression: 1. Increase side-bend repetitions by one each week and gradually increase the amount of time each bend is held.

2. Increase to two or three minutes the amount of time you hold each vertical hang. For best results perform both exercises two or three times daily. Once the deviations are corrected perform the side bends to both sides.

C. Posture Deviation: Feet Pointed Out with Ankles Sagging In

Exercise: **Edge Walking**

Purpose: To stretch the muscles and connective tissues on the outside of the ankles and strengthen those on the inside.

Action: While standing with your shoes off, rotate your feet so that the inside edges are off the floor and all of the weight is on the outside edges. Learn to balance yourself on the outer edges of your feet for about 30 seconds. Then take ten steps walking on the outer edges of your feet. Perform three repetitions, beginning with the 30-second balance and followed by the ten-step walk. Use a padded or carpeted surface. For best results exercise two or three times daily.

Progression: Over a period of three to four weeks gradually increase the number of steps to 30. In addition, when you walk or run, concentrate on keeping your toes pointed directly to the front.

NOTE: If you have chronic ankle problems, consult your physician before using the above exercise.

D. Posture Deviation: Head Carried Forward of Shoulders (Hang-dog Head)

Exercise: **Isometric Neck Push**

Purpose: To strengthen the muscles on the back of the neck.

Action: Interlace fingers of both hands behind your head. Press head backward against the resistance offered by your hands and arms. Hold for a count of six and do three repetitions. For best results repeat two or three times daily.

Progression: Over a period of three to four weeks increase to ten repetitions, holding for a count of six.

E. Posture Deviation: Rounding of Upper Back with Forward Shoulders (Dowager's Hump)

Exercise: **Arm Fling**

Purpose: To stretch the muscles of the chest and strengthen the muscles of the upper back.

Action: See description of exercise, page 166, under the intermediate level in the chapter titled The Later Years.

Progression: Start with 20 repetitions and increase to 50 over a three- to four-week period. For best results repeat two or three times daily.

F. Posture Deviation: Forward Pelvic Tilt, Causing a Protruding Stomach, Rearward Incline of the Trunk, and an Exaggerated Spinal Curve in the Lower Back

Exercises: **1. Bent-Knee Curl**
2. Knee-to-Chest Pull
3. Arm Fling

Action: See pages 23, 64, and 166 respectively for descriptions.

Progression: 1. Bent-Knee Curl. Do this at same level you are working in the Basic Five. However, perform exercise at least six days a week at a slow cadence.

2. Knee-to-Chest Pull. As a flexibility or posture exercise begin by performing three repetitions two or three times each day for the first week. Hold each pull for a count of ten. Exercise at least five times a week, preferably every day. Increase number of repetitions to ten over a three- to four-week period.

3. Arm Fling. Start with 20 repetitions and increase to 50 over a three- to four-week period. For best results repeat two or three times daily.

CHAPTER 12

Tips for
Better Performance

The right clothing and shoes plus proper breathing and proper running techniques all benefit your performance and conditioning while protecting your health. For those reasons, it's important that you observe the following tips:

1. *A proper warm-up* is essential before beginning to exercise strenuously, especially if you are over thirty. As a rule of thumb, the older you are, the more warm-up time you need to protect yourself against aches and pains.

2. *Proper clothing* is loose and comfortable to keep from hindering blood circulation or restricting your movement. *Do not wear rubberized or plastic clothing,* for the evaporation of sweat, which is necessary to maintain proper body temperature, is curtailed by nonporous clothing. In fact, rubberized or plastic clothing may cause the body temperature to fluctuate up and down dangerously, thus bringing on heat exhaustion or a heat stroke.

Underclothing should be supportive: jockey shorts or preferably an athletic supporter for men, to prevent sag, and bras for women. It's also recommended that women wear either cotton panties or panties with a cotton crotch. Some synthetic fabrics have caused vaginal irritation in some women, especially when worn while exercising.

3. *When you exercise* is up to you. There is no bad time as far as the body is concerned except for the first hour after eating. We recommend early morning, before breakfast and your shower, because it is too easy to make excuses later in the day. Incidentally, if you are having trouble dieting, you'll find that exercising just before eating or instead of eating will help dull your appetite.

4. *Where you exercise* deserves some consideration. A padded or carpeted floor is always recommended for exercising, especially for running in place. Outdoors, running on tracks and smooth grassy fields are most recommended, but any place will do. If possible, try to avoid running on hard surfaces such as concrete and asphalt for the first few weeks. If this is impossible, then take more time at a slower pace to allow the muscles, tendons, and bones of the lower legs to get used to the shock of running on hard surfaces. Wear a good pair of running shoes and, in the beginning, two pairs of athletic socks.

5. *Good shoes* are your best protection when running, and there are a number of good running shoes on the market today. The better shoes are expensive but recommended if you plan on doing a lot of running. Here are some things to look for in making your selection:

• A running shoe is comparatively much lighter than ordinary footwear. However, the lightest and flimsiest running shoes are for speed runners and short distances. For CR conditioning, you will be taking long, slow runs, and therefore your shoes should be more substantial. This is important in order to provide better protection for your feet and lower legs.

• Carefully inspect the sole, the most important part of the shoe. (The upper part of the shoe, despite all the decorations, is only there to hold the sole to your foot.) Squeeze and bend the sole. There should be some cushioning, but it shouldn't be soft. The purpose of the cushioning is to absorb the shock—if it's too soft, it can't do the job. A higher-density rubber will be better and will last longer. The sole should be fairly stiff over the back two thirds with good flexibility in the front one third. It's the front one third that bends as you roll forward at toe-off in the running stride.

• Choose shoes that fit the outline of your feet as nearly as possible. Trace the outline of the shoe sole on a piece of paper to see if your foot will fit within the outline. (Note: Take special care in choosing shoes made abroad. The sizes are often different from American sizes.)

• Try *both* shoes on, wearing the socks that you plan to wear when running. Walk in them and test for feel. The shoes should immediately feel comfortable. If not, try another pair. Jump up and down to see if the sole cushions the shock in both the soles and heels. Move your feet around inside the shoes and feel for ridges or seams that may cause irritation and blisters. Your feet should not feel cramped—if they do, get a larger size because you want support without cramping. The top edge of the heel should not put pressure on the Achilles tendon. (Note: Some experienced runners don't wear socks, and that is all right. However, when you first start running, wear socks as protection against shock and blisters. After your feet and legs are in shape, you can try running without socks.)

• If you normally require arch supports in your shoes, then you will also need them in your running shoes. Do not rely exclusively on the arch supports that come in the shoes.

• Don't buy running shoes for anyone else, and don't let someone choose shoes for you. Each person must personally go through the fitting procedure. Remember that the shoes are going to help protect your feet from the thousands of small shocks in thousands of running steps. The shoes you choose are most helpful in preventing some of the nagging injuries that some joggers experience.

6. *The avoidance of injuries* when running is possible by understanding the causes of the two most common problems: *shin splints*—pain on the front or sides of the lower legs—and the *sore Achilles tendon.* The shin splint, which is inflammation of the muscles that control movement of the foot, appears to be the result of running on hard surfaces before muscles are properly conditioned, fallen arches without arch supports, improper body alignment from lower-back strain, and poor running habits.

The sore Achilles tendon is usually the result of poor conditioning. The exercises in the flexibility and posture sections of this book will help prevent problems with the Achilles tendon. Note: If you do flexibility and stretching exercises immediately after running, this will help prevent muscular tightness that may cause injury the next day.

7. *Running correctly* is a matter too often explained simplistically. Generally, you are told that you should run heel to toe— that the heel should strike the ground first and that you roll your weight along the sole and push off with your toes. This simplistic explanation results in the runner making two major errors: First, he stomps his heel into the ground in trying to follow the heel-to-toe running method; and second, he tries to run off his toes when the bones and muscles are not designed to take that kind of shock. Actually, when you watch the proper foot movement

in running, it is not a rolling motion like a rocker rolling forward. Instead, the heel strikes the ground just before the ball of the foot, almost like a flat-footed glide step.

One additional problem that often needs correcting is getting the runner to keep the toes pointed straight ahead. Toe-out running is a cause of strain and soreness in the feet and lower legs. To break the habit of toe-out running and walking, exaggerate and try toe-in or "pigeon-toe" walking and running.

Another relatively common fault of beginning runners is toe-in running, which may be corrected by using the Edge Walking exercise on page 221.

8. *Breathing* is such a natural function that we don't realize that it can become a problem for some people when they begin to exercise. They tend to hold their breath, especially when trying to overcome heavy resistances such as in push-ups and pull-ups. Contrary to what many people believe, holding your breath doesn't give you more strength. Instead, it can create a hazard.

The physiological condition brought on by holding your breath while exercising is called the Valsalva effect. What happens is that the abdominal muscles contract and the glottis (in the throat) closes. This causes a build up of pressure within the inner rib cage and abdominal areas. This, in turn, inhibits the venous return of blood to the heart, causing the blood pressure to fall in the arteries. Then there is a reflex increase in the heart rate, a surge of venous blood into the heart, causing the blood pressure to increase in the pulmonary arteries. This increase can be dangerous for someone with an undetected weakness in the pulmonary arteries.

At West Point we instruct the cadets that they should inhale and exhale during each repetition of an exercise. The general rule when exercising is to exhale on effort, i.e., when you are pushing up from the floor or pulling up to the bar, and then inhale as you lower your body. When running, breathing should be deep and rhythmical. Short, shallow breathing can cause dizziness through hyperventilation. If you feel winded, breathe deeper —not faster.

It is important to breathe properly. The muscles need oxygen when they contract. The brain needs oxygen to maintain consciousness. If you feel lightheaded or dizzy when exercising, check your breathing.

CHAPTER 13

Lifetime Sports

West Point's athletic philosophy was established by General Douglas MacArthur when he became the superintendent in 1919. He had concluded from his experience in World War I that those officers who had taken part in organized sports made the best soldiers. He considered them to be the most dependable, self-disciplined, hardy, and courageous officers he had. As a result, General MacArthur initiated an athletic philosophy that is followed to this day and can be best described as, "Every cadet an athlete."

Out of this philosophy has developed a sophisticated and balanced physical education program. Its base is the personal conditioning program that is the basis for this book. Cadets are individually responsible throughout their four years for both progress and maintenance in personal conditioning.

In addition cadets are required to participate in athletics at one of three levels: intercollegiate, club squad, or intramural. Participation goes on throughout the year. For example, a varsity football player might play intramural basketball in the winter and club-squad rugby in the spring. As you can see from the list on the following page, most of the sports are vigorous.

INTERCOLLEGIATE ATHLETICS

Fall	Winter		Spring
Cross-Country	Basketball	Rifle	Baseball
Football	Fencing	Skiing	Golf
150-lb Football	Gymnastics	Squash	Lacrosse
Soccer	Hockey	Swimming	Outdoor Track
Water Polo	Indoor Track	Volleyball	Tennis
	Pistol	Wrestling	

CLUB SPORTS

Bowling Team
Cycling Team
Handball Team
Horseback Riding Team
Judo Team
Karate Team
Marathon Team
Mountaineering Team
Orienteering Team

Outdoor Sportsman Club
Rugby Team
Sailing Team
SCUBA Club
Skeet and Trap Team
Sport Parachute Team
Team Handball Team
Triathlon Team

INTRAMURAL ATHLETICS

Fall	Winter	Spring	
Flickerball	Basketball	Badminton	Racquetball
Football	Boxing	Basketball	Softball
Soccer	Handball	(three-man)	Super Jock
Track	Squash	Boat Racing	Decathlon
Triathlon	Swimming	Bowling	Team Handball
	Volleyball	Cross-Country	Tennis
	Wrestling	Floor Hockey	Touch Football
		Golf	Track
		Lacrosse	Water Polo

And there is a third part to the program. During the cadets' first year there are five required courses that help develop basic physical abilities: survival swimming and gymnastics, which are coed, and combatives, which include self-defense for the women and boxing and wrestling for the men. During their last three years upper-class cadets concentrate on developing skills in sports that they can use for the remainder of their lives. We call these elective activities lifetime sports or carry-over sports. Their purpose is to help cadets develop the habit of being physically active throughout their lives. Every cadet is taught five or six different sport activities to carry over into his career. Since officers will be stationed in different areas with widely varying climates, we recommend that they learn both indoor and outdoor lifetime activities. The list includes:

LIFETIME SPORTS

Aerobics	Skiing
Badminton	Squash
Bowling	Strength development
Boxing	Survival swimming
Golf	Tennis
Gymnastics	Unarmed combat
Handball	Volleyball
Ice skating	Water-safety instruction
Racquetball	Wrestling
Scuba	

Why do we teach lifetime sports?

We know that people who participate in sports throughout their lives are more likely to keep in good condition through exercising and running. Also, sports help maintain agility, coordination, and grace. However, cadets are cautioned against dependence on sports for maintaining basic conditioning.

Cadets also go the textbook and lecture route in physical education, which means that by graduation they can literally prescribe their own conditioning needs. They know that no sport is as comprehensive and efficient in conditioning the primary muscle groups as the Basic Five. Furthermore, they understand that you can't simply substitute a sport for cardiorespiratory conditioning on a one-to-one basis. For example, if you discontinue running two or three times a week, then you would have to play a vigorous sport four or five times a week to maintain the same level of fitness.

Unfortunately, some sports, like golf and bowling, do not count as vigorous sports. Both are enjoyable, but a 150-pound person will use only some 3.5 calories per minute at bowling and 4.0 to 5.5 calories per minute at golf, depending upon whether you are playing with a foursome or twosome. As a reference point you should consider a vigorous activity one that will cause a 150-pound person to use at least 7 calories per minute of actual participation.

Here are some lifetime, or carry-over, sports that we teach at West Point. Because they are more vigorous, they are more beneficial to health and conditioning.

Badminton: Although badminton can be played at various

levels of intensity by all age groups, it's a vigorous racquet game when played by well-matched and skilled opponents. When played expertly, badminton requires quick stops and starts and skillful racquet work. Your arms and legs must be well-conditioned, and your cardiorespiratory endurance is important. A 150-pound person will use 6 to 10 calories per minute depending upon the level of skill and whether it is recreational or competitive play.

Bicycling: A good sport for development of cardiorespiratory fitness. It can be useful and helpful for all ages. There are even three-wheeled cycles for use in later years that are popular at some retirement communities. But for some, particularly the young, leisurely cycling may not be enough to develop CR fitness. If you want to know how fast you must cycle in order to benefit your CR system, check your pulse. Use the same procedure as for the Walk/Run Plan. Note that you should not attempt to measure your pulse while moving. A 150-pounder will burn from 5 to 11 calories per minute depending upon speed from 5.5 mph to 13 mph on level ground.

Handball: A vigorous game involving the entire body, and a good activity for building and maintaining CR endurance. The younger you learn it, the better. It's not advisable for men and women in their fifties and sixties to take up handball if they have never played before. As with most lifetime sports it's more fun to play against someone close to your own ability level. A 150-pound person will use about 10 calories per minute playing handball.

Ice skating: An enjoyable sport for all ages that exercises your arms, legs, and trunk muscles. Skating's usefulness depends on the level and intensity of the individual skater. It's doubtful that the beginner will receive any CR benefits, but skilled figure and speed skaters will stress their CR systems. A skilled 150-pound person will burn from 6 to 10 calories per minute depending upon whether the skating is moderate or vigorous in intensity.

Racquetball: Like handball this is a vigorous game, but unlike handball you are using only one arm to strike the ball. Handball purists look down their noses at racquetball, claiming that it requires no skill, but they are wrong. We encourage cadets to learn both sports. Racquetball has several advantages for the beginning player. It's a relatively easy game to learn and often an enjoyable game the first time on the court. Unlike handball, racquetball can be learned as early as the age of 9 and 10, and also by people in their fifties who have been active in other sports. Racquetball is also a great alternate game for frustrated tennis players who cannot play outside because of the weather. Anyone who has played another racquet sport will pick up the game easily. This is a great CR activity. A 150-pound person will use about 10 calories per minute playing racquetball.

Scuba diving: This is different from most lifetime sports. Different because scuba diving doesn't contribute much to your physical fitness. However, you must be in good physical condition in order to participate safely. You also have to be expert and follow all of the rules of safety because a mistake can cost your life. The best physical conditioning for scuba diving comes from swimming.

Skiing—Alpine and Cross-Country: If you are like most skiers in America, you are a weekend skier. You must therefore maintain good muscular strength and endurance, especially in your legs, to prevent being involved in accidents. Alpine skiing can be learned at any age, and as long as you stay in shape for it, you can continue to ski as long as you wish. It is relatively easy to learn with proper instruction, and competitive cross-country skiers are among the best conditioned athletes in the world. Competitive skiing requires great muscular endurance as well as CR endurance. Since you can decide how fast you want to go when you are cross-country skiing, you can participate in this activity at any age. The 150-pound person will use about 10 calories per minute when participating in either alpine or cross-country skiing.

Squash: This is a racquet game that requires agility. Also arm, shoulder, wrist, and grip strength are important, and it's great for CR conditioning when played by equally matched, skilled players. Squash is probably easier to learn than handball but not as easy as racquetball. Women with strong wrists can play squash very well. A 150-pound person who is reasonably skilled will burn up about 10 calories per minute playing squash.

Swimming: Swimming is one of the best forms of physical conditioning, but it must be vigorous. Many of us don't swim well enough to maintain a pace that will contribute to our CR conditioning—which means attaining a heart rate above 65 percent of maximum and keeping it there for at least five minutes. Swimming is best learned at a young age, the younger the better, and once you develop the skill you can swim at any age. A 150-pound person can burn up about 10 calories per minute when swimming the crawl stroke at the rate of 50 yards per minute.

Tennis: Tennis is a game that can be learned and played at all age levels from under 10 into the later years for those who have remained active. As with other sports, the conditioning value of tennis increases as you become more skillful. A youngster at the beginning level of tennis may need some other form of activity in order to help grow and develop an adequate level of muscular strength. Tennis players will play a better game if they also participate in the Walk/Run and BBC programs. A 150-pound person will use between 7 and 10 calories per minute depending on whether the game is at the recreational or competitive level.

RATING LIFETIME SPORTS IN THE ORDER THEY PROMOTE OVERALL PHYSICAL FITNESS

1. Bicycling
2. Swimming
3. Handball
4. Racquetball
5. Squash
6. Cross-country skiing
7. Ice skating
8. Alpine skiing
9. Tennis
10. Badminton

CHAPTER 14

For Women Only

Would you say that most of the following statements are true or false?

• Athletic women have fewer complications during pregnancy and childbirth.

• At a recent Olympiad, nearly one third of the women athletes competed during menstruation.

• A woman's reproductive organs are better protected than a man's.

• After giving birth to one or more children women have gone on to win medals and set new records in athletic competition.

• Lifting weights will improve a woman's figure.

If you believe that any of the above statements are false, then you are perpetuating the myth that women are frail, delicate creatures. All the statements above are true, for, in fact, women have sturdy, well-designed bodies with durable and efficient internal mechanisms. The individual and institutional prejudices that handicap women are based almost entirely on myths and medical folklore, which have now been disproved.

Menstruation and Physical Performance

Old wives' tales about menstruation have existed for thousands of years. Even today many people consider "that time of the month" as a kind of illness that women must suffer, a period during which their physical activities must be restricted. But medical literature and research support an altogether different attitude.

Recent medical studies find that women who are physically active as a matter of routine have fewer menstrual complaints,

234

including chronic headaches, fatigue, and cramps. These studies also find that exercise more than anything else will help prevent menstrual cramps by increasing blood circulation and releasing muscular tensions. The best exercises are bending and stretching, which work the muscles of the abdomen and lower back.

Studies also show that menstruation has no affect on athletic performance. Women have won Olympic medals during every phase of the menstrual cycle. There are some exceptions—women adversely affected during menses—but medical research is in general agreement that if a woman is normally healthy, neither her physical nor mental efficiency needs to be affected in the biological cycle.

Increasingly fewer and fewer high schools and colleges are excusing women from physical education during the menstrual period. Instead, full participation in athletics is encouraged during all phases of menstruation. When the first women cadets were admitted to the Academy, we felt it prudent to have medical advice on the matter because of the very strenuous physical activity of the first eight weeks.

To advise us on how physical stress would affect the menstrual cycle of women cadets, we engaged as a consultant a woman who has done numerous studies involving the effects of physical exercise on menstruation and pregnancy—Evalyn S. Gendel, M.D., an associate director for the Maternal and Child Health Bureau of the Kansas State Department of Health and Environment.

The Academy administration had decided that in fairness to both men and women cadets our attitude would be that women can do anything men can do unless it's proven that they can't. Dr. Gendel in turn agreed that the 118 women entering West Point should be expected to match the same high level of effort in physical performance as the men with no "time-out" for the menstrual period. And that is what happened. Women cadets have followed the same training schedule as the men regardless of their menstrual cycle, and during the entire eight weeks of strenuous training only one woman asked to be excused from training because of menstrual cramps.

Pregnancy and Physical Activity

There are pregnant women who work in the home or at their

jobs until minutes before they take a cab to the hospital's delivery room, and there is a woman rodeo rider who roped calves and rode bucking broncs into the eighth month of her pregnancy. (Her doctor said the only real danger would be if she got kicked in the stomach by a horse.) How much activity any individual woman should have during pregnancy is a matter to be settled between each woman and her physician. However, it appears that the need for most women to be treated delicately is another myth.

In one study of 172 women athletes who had 184 pregnancies and deliveries, two-thirds continued to compete in sports events into the first two or three months of pregnancy. Most stopped by the fourth month, not because of discomfort but because their performance dropped. On the other hand, many women, both athletes and nonathletes, routinely participate in recreational activities into their eighth and ninth months of pregnancy.

In other studies, including one by Dr. Gendel, it's been found that women who have a history of maintaining physical conditioning have fewer complications either during pregnancy or during delivery. For those women who have backache, fatigue, kidney, and pelvis problems, Dr. Gendel has successfully prescribed physical conditioning both before and during pregnancy. Dr. Gendel herself spent the first eight months of one pregnancy taking ski lessons.

Furthermore, childbirth appears to be a positive factor in the life of some women athletes, for a number of top-ranking women athletes have become Olympic champions after having a child. The most recent example was at the Montreal Olympiad, when a Polish mother of three set a new world record in winning the 400-meter gold medal in track.

Conditioning in the Menopausal Years

Another myth that hurts women is the belief that it's wise to take it easy when you approach menopause. As a result, many women let themselves go—become sedentary, over-eat, and put on excess fat which makes the menopausal years a more difficult period.

In fact women who have been physically active before menopause should continue to be so throughout their menopause and beyond, and those women who have been sedentary should get started in an exercise and diet program appropriate for their age.

The benefits of physical conditioning during menopause include reducing muscular tensions and backaches through the Basic Five and flexibility exercises. Furthermore, the Walk/Run program will help to give women the good health and vigor to deal with other symptoms of menopause.

Iron Deficiency

One common belief—that women frequently suffer from iron deficiency—turned out to be true, as we have discovered at West Point. About four weeks after the first contingent of women cadets arrived at the Academy, twenty-four underwent a medical examination because of sub-par physical performance. Fifteen of them showed iron deficiency, a cause of unnecessary fatigue, which can easily be prevented.

The prevention of iron deficiency depends simply on ingesting proper nutrients or iron supplements. The recommended daily allowance for young women is 18 mg. of iron per day, except during menstruation, when women may need double or triple amounts.

Some Sources of Iron

Food	Amount	Iron (mg.)
Pork liver	3 oz.	17.7
Lamb liver	3 oz.	12.6
Chicken liver	3 oz.	8.4
Fried oysters	3 oz.	6.9
Beef liver	3 oz.	6.6
Dried apricots	½ cup	5.5
Roast turkey	3 oz.	5.1
Prune juice	½ cup	4.9
Pork chop	3 oz.	4.5
Beef	3 oz.	4.2
Beans (kidney or baked)	½ cup	3.0
Hamburger	3 oz.	3.0
Raisins	½ cup	2.5
Lima beans	½ cup	2.5

Iron from foods of animal origin is more effective than iron from vegetables or fruit because the iron in meat is absorbed twice as efficiently.

What Women Should Know About Weight Training

It's not necessary that every woman go in for weight lifting, but she should overcome her fears and prejudices, because weight training has specific benefits for women.

First, weight training is an efficient way to improve your performance in sports whether your game is golf, tennis, or swimming. It's the consensus of experts that the advantage of Eastern European women in the Montreal Olympiad was their weight training, which increased their muscular strength and endurance.

Another benefit for women is unexpected. Weight training is an excellent way to develop a trim, well-contoured figure. Professional actresses have used weight lifting to improve their figures.

The fears about weight training are mostly myths. One such fear is that lifting weights will give women bulky muscles like a man's. This isn't true and has never been supported by scientific data. At West Point we tested this out to our satisfaction when we were preparing for the admittance of women cadets. In one study we placed a group of 20 high school women on an intensive weight-training program for eight weeks. All increased their strength substantially, but not one developed anything that could be remotely described as bulky muscles.

The fear that weight training will masculinize women—lower her voice, change her walk, and turn her into a physical freak— is absolutely ridiculous. We're all learning as women athletes receive more and more attention in the media that despite their intense physical training, women athletes are no less attractive than other women.

Any woman considering heavy weight training should do so only under professional supervision. On the other hand, Chapter 10, BBC (Beyond Basic Conditioning) for All Ages, contains a series of lightweight exercises using dumbbells. These exercises can be done in the home and are of particular benefit to women who are active in recreational sports because our studies and experience at West Point have shown us that American women lack muscular conditioning in at least three important areas:

1. Arm-shoulder-girdle weakness was apparent in the difficulty young women have in doing push-ups and their inability to do pull-ups. The arm-shoulder girdle includes chest, back, shoulder, and upper-arm muscles, all important in appearance, maintaining posture, and upper-body strength required for such activities as swimming, tennis and golf.

2. Poor grip strength was discovered when women cadets found it difficult to carry a ten-pound rifle while running and doing rifle exercises. Grip strength is important to anyone who wants to participate in sports that involve holding an implement such as a tennis racquet, golf club, or bat. Also, our studies show that there is a significant correlation between grip strength and other strength measurements that we have taken.

3. Poor development of trunk muscles was obvious. When young women tried to do push-ups, they couldn't keep their bodies straight. Some young women turned out to be awkward when it came to running or jumping, and this is another indication of weak trunk muscles. It is trunk muscles that stabilize the pelvic girdle, which is part of the foundation for almost all physical activities.

If these characteristics are common to most American women, and it's likely that they are, the weaknesses can be efficiently corrected through the Basic Five and, if necessary, the BBC.